Canine Field Medicine

By Sid Gustafson, DVM

MW00856395

Adventure Medical Kits
BE SAFE

Canine Field Medicine / Sid Gustafson DVM --1st ed.—
ISBN 978-0-692-78739-7
1. Medicine—Canine—Wounds and Injuries—Treatment. 2. Dogs—Diseases—Treatment. 3. Veterinary Medicine—Canine I. Title.

Published by
Tender Corporation
944 Industrial Park Road
Littleton, New Hampshire 03561

adventuremedicalkits.com

Design and layout by Alaina Delabruere.
Instructional photos by Steven Drake.

Item # 4000-1520

The first rule of medicine is ***first, do no harm.*** In all cases of canine injury and illness, it is always recommended you take your dog to your veterinarian for a professional medical assessment. In the meantime, this text will guide you how to proceed in the absence of professional veterinary care. The author accepts no liability for suggested treatment guidelines suggested herein. Successful treatment is predicated upon accurate assessment. It is important that the guardian read this guide in its entirety before traveling out of the reach of veterinary care with their faithful companion, *Canis familiaris*. The information contained herein regarding pet health and field medical treatments should be discussed at length with your dog's personal veterinarian before venturing afield. All of the advice offered here is predicated upon the previously established valid Veterinarian Client Patient Relationship, the triad of you, your dog, and your veterinarian. The Veterinarian/Client/Patient/Relationship is important to maintain as your dog's health changes with time. The ethical care and successful treatment of your pet is based upon a *bona fide* relationship with your veterinarian.

CONTENTS

For Freckles and Spek and Nate and Jake and the billions of other individual creatures who have merged with mankind …

I would like to thank the multitude of dogs and horses that taught and comforted me throughout my life. Never have I been alone. My animals endowed me with an appreciation of nature, myself, and the world.

In the end, we must all understand and rely upon each other to survive.

Veterinary medical thanks to Drs. Randolph Scott, Doug Hepper, Jeff Osborn, Haven Leavitt, Catherine Lindblad, Ed Ketel, Charlie Noland, Barr Gustafson, and Raymond Walter Gustafson for their veterinary review, friendship, support, assistance, and relentless professional care through the decades to animals of all sorts.

Personal thanks to my children Connor and Nina who taught me the truest meaning of compassion towards animals.

About the Author

Born Under the Chinook Arch in Conrad, Montana, Sid Gustafson had the great fortune to be raised by dogs and horses on a ranch along the Two Medicine River on the Blackfeet Indian Reservation. His veterinarian father and artistic mother, along with four younger siblings ensconced him with an animal life on the land. Sid's childhood dog Cinder and mare Becky were responsible for Sid's inherent connection to domestic animals. Sid cherished his childhood immersed in the Montana animal life when he was able and willing to learn from animals and their guardians alike. There is an age when a child is able to learn from the animals themselves, and Sid lived that age fully. His teenage summers were spent horseback on the largest cattle ranch in America. Sheep, swine, grizzly bears, wolves, cattle and bison surrounded him beside all those horses and dogs. Clearly, horse and dog are part of Sid's family.

Healing courses Dr. Sid's blood. In this medical guide, he shares his healing art with all those who treasure their dog's health and prosperity. Sid matriculated from Washington State University in 1979 a Doctor of Veterinary Medicine. In addition to practicing veterinary medicine in Bozeman, Montana throughout his professional career, he teaches equine behavior at the University of Guelph.

Sid provides behavioral consultations to resolve behavioral, health, and training issues in dogs, horses, and other domestic species. If you are having trouble managing the behavior of your dog or horse, Dr. Gustafson can help you fulfill your companion's behavioral needs to facilitate the development of a willing partnership to resolve unwelcome behaviors. While many view indentured servitude as the appropriate human/dog construct, Dr. Gustafson knows that it is willing partnerships that create the ideal relationships between dogs and their guardians.

Dr. Gustafson is an animal welfare advocate. He has written extensively for the New York Times regarding the health and welfare of racehorses across America. In addition to being a diverse social commentator and teacher regarding the human/animal bond, Sid is a prominent Montana fiction writer and novelist. He is the author of *HORSES THEY RODE*,

High Plains Novel of the Year in 2007. His most recent non-fiction is *Horse Behavior, The Nature of Horses*. His debut novel published in New York in 2003, *Prisoners of Flight*, is a literary exploration of the animal in man. His third novel, *Swift Dam*, will be published the summer of 2016. His latest short fiction can be read in the *Montana Quarterly Magazine*. More information about Dr. Gustafson's animal life and times can be found at www.sidgustafson.com or on his blog at http://sidgustafson.blogspot.com

In addition to practicing veterinary medicine for decades, Dr. Gustafson teaches animal behavior for the University of Guelph. This book provides information regarding the principles of canine behavior as they apply to canine field medicine. Restraint contributes 90% to the effectiveness of field medicine, and willing restraint is always best. The narrative is designed to teach and then assist canine guardians to effectively respond to manage canine emergencies and illnesses they may encounter in the field where veterinary care is not available. It is also a concise guide on how to keep your dog healthy and to endure the rigors of outdoor adventure.

Dogs stand in judgment at the gates of my heaven.

PREFACE

Canine Behavior

Included in this medical guide is the information necessary to keep your dog optimally healthy so as to withstand the rigors of backcountry travel and wilderness adventure. Please read the book in its entirety before you embark. Prevention and preparation will avoid the need for backcountry medical care.

Dr. Gustafson's guidelines for the resolution of illness and accidents have saved countless canine lives when administered in a knowing and practiced fashion. Included is the knowledge necessary to evaluate the seriousness of your dog's illness or injury, so please study this book before you venture into the wild with your faithful friend. The preventive health and first-response accident information is intended to be an adjunct and prelude to appropriate veterinary care when it becomes available.

Outdoor recreation with dogs involves risk. To enjoy a safe backcountry experience with your animal companion, learn as much as you can from this book. The information presented here, if followed, will teach how to manage a lifetime of health and prevention, avoiding the need for veterinary care of all types. Prepare for the unexpected. Life is fragile. In your dog's best interest, enjoy reading *Canine Field Medicine* before you embark into the wild. Dr. Gustafson is an entertaining writer.

In the meantime, develop a willing partnership with your dog. Instill the confidence to allow him or her to accept handling for a thorough examination of the major body parts on a routine basis. It is imperative that your dog accept treatment in order for treatment to be successfully administered. Practice examining your dog ahead of your outdoor adventure, please. Know all of his or her normal parameters and vital signs. Deviations from normal indicate medical issues are developing which are best addressed sooner rather than later. A stitch in time saves nine.

Know thy dog!

Basic dog responsibilities:

Know your dog's normal temperature, heart rate, and respiratory rate, as well as the normal color, smell, and feel of the mucous membranes in the mouth (wet and warm, clean smelling). Train your dog to make it a good deal for him or her to allow restraint and handling in order to attend to any possible medical needs that may arise in the outback future.

Effective initial treatment and safe transport of an injured dog to a veterinarian are critical elements of field medicine. Successful treatment of many of the injuries and conditions described herein may be beyond the scope of your ability, so appreciate both your limitations and abilities. Injuries and illnesses often eventually require professional medical care for resolution, so follow up with your veterinarian for significant issues. The method and efficiency in which you handle the problem in its early stages can determine how the dog recovers. To successfully and effectively administer dog first aid requires knowledge, preparation, and a dog that can be willingly handled and treated. Please develop a willing partnership with your dog that facilitates handling and treatment of minor issues. Again, take the time to train you dog to undergo a thorough examination of her paws, legs, groin, tongue, teeth, ears, rear, and tail. Get a handle on your dog's normal respiratory rate and heart rate, as well as the normal wet and warm feel and color of the gums. Understand your dog's digestive and urinary functions, and pay attention to all eliminations, please, noting any change in consistency, color, or frequency. Most backcountry malaise and illness offer plenty of warning signs, if only the guardian pays careful attention to their dog's vital signs and behavior.

The information presented here is based on my personal experiences during thirty-five years of veterinary practice, and before that, twenty years assisting my veterinarian father Under the Chinook Arch of northcentral Montana, The Rocky Mountain Front, an ancient dog country. My friends of the Blackfeet Nation are descendants of the original North American dog people. They taught me the nature of dogs and horses, and demonstrated that the preferred relationship between humans and animals is a mutually beneficial relationship. These North Americans brought their dogs with them, and their dogs help them survive every step of the way.

My family of dogs, people, and horses ventures into the Bob Marshall Wilderness each summer to get the feel of how it might have been before Manifest Destiny changed North America. Breaks from the world of technology are increasingly welcome and ameliorative for dog, man, and horse.

The canine field medical procedures and related preventive-health recommendations herein are derived from my own and my father's experiences as outback veterinarians.

Sid Gustafson, DVM   *December 2015*

Dedicated to the memory and refined healing arts promoted by Raymond Walter "Rib" Gustafson, DVM 1925-2014, throughout his illustrious and textured veterinary career Under the Chinook Arch of Northcentral Montana, that ancient cusp of culture and geography located under the Medicine Line between the Golden Triangle and the Bob Marshall Wilderness, the last true outback of continental America.

PART I   PREREQUISITES TO FIRST AID

1   Accident Prevention

Leashes

Many injuries occur when your dog leaves your side to play and explore. Keep track of your pet, especially in new or unfamiliar environments. It is preferable to keep your dog within your field of vision, or, short of that, within earshot. Your dog's safety is best served when he is trained to come promptly when called, even in the heat of excitement. Quick responses to your basic commands of come, sit, heel, and stay are essential for your pet's safety. Prompt and willing obedience will help keep your dog away from threatening situations. A dog's world can be overwhelming, and even the best-trained individuals may exhibit selective hearing under intense circumstances. The simple use of a leash may be one of your best tools in preventing injuries. If your pet is on a leash, you are able to manage threatening situations. Off-leash travel is highly desirable for a variety of reasons, but when approaching unfamiliar situations, leashing your dog is always the best policy.

In addition to its use in controlling your dog in possibly harmful circumstances, the leash is also an important piece of field medical equipment. It allows you to restrain your injured dog in order to properly examine and treat him. Some dogs will instinctively run and hide when injured; the leash not only keeps them by you, it also prevents further injury. Accustom your dog to a leash and use it when approaching dangerous situations or unfamiliar areas. Make sure the collar fits properly and has your name, address, and phone number on it in case the dog gets lost or runs away. This identification is a sign of a conscientious owner and will help ensure medical treatment, if necessary. Additionally, a rabies tag can direct your pet to his own personal veterinarian. A client/dog/veterinary relationship is important. Your veterinarian can enhance your canine field medical kit with medicines specific to your pet's needs once she appreciates your dog's health status and your ability to assess health and administer first aid.

Know Your Environment

It is important to be informed about the terrain and wildlife of the areas you plan to visit. Get information about the animals, plants, and approved uses of the areas you explore, as well as current or previous activities in the area, such as mining, logging, trapping, hunting, poisoning, beetle killing, or weed spraying.

Pay close attention to the environment when you hike with your dog. Avoid conflicts with all wildlife, especially those animals that may impact your dog's health, such as skunks, porcupines, bears, coyotes, wolves, moose, and wolverines. If you do encounter a wild animal, retreat with your leashed dog and allow the wild animal her deserved space. Keep in mind that spring is a critical season for newborn wildlife and backcountry wildlife are particularly sensitive to encroachment by people and their pets during this time. Always give wildlife their privacy and distance, please.

Rabies

Skunks, foxes, bats, dogs, raccoons, and other mammals can transmit rabies by biting. Raccoons and others can transmit distemper, also. It is essential to have your dog routinely examined by your veterinarian and protected against rabies as required and needed. After the first two vaccinations, titers can be taken annually to determine protection of your dog, thus avoiding relentless vaccination protocols if that is not your preference. Keep your pet's rabies vaccination or titer results current. Rabies vaccinations are recommended every three years after the initial one-year immunization dose. Rabies is fatal for most mammals, including man, and not a pleasant way to go as Old Yeller and Cujo have attested. Veterinarians are required to administer rabies vaccinations and perform rabies titers, and this visit is a good time to develop a relationship with your other family doctor.

Rabid animals often exhibit unusual behavior. Rabid wildlife and bats lose their fear of people and dogs, and may bite recklessly when approached or handled. As well, rabid animals may appear to be normal. They may or may not salivate and slobber and are not necessarily afraid of water (hydrophobic). Rabid animals often make weird vocalizations, and so you should listen for this key sign. The affected make funny noises because their larynx and vocal chords become afflicted with the virus as the virus reaches in to capture the brain. This may be the first thing noticed, a funny bark, a weird meow, an unwholesome nicker or neigh. Foxes, raccoons, and skunks with porcupine quills are almost always rabid. Deranged by the rabies virus, wild animals sometimes attack porcupines or fail to avoid them, which is out of character for normal wildlife (but apparently not normal dogs). If the wild animal has quills in his nose, you can assume he is rabid. (This is fortunately *not* the case with domestic dogs, whose ancient self-preservation strategies have been bred out of them.)

If you, or your dog, are bitten by a wild mammal, the possibility of rabies transmission should be discussed with your veterinarian and physician. The incubation period for rabies is weeks to months or longer, a long time to wait and worry if the situation is not medically investigated by the proper doctors and public health authorities, please.

Dogs can also contract distemper, plague, and other more obscure illnesses from tick, insect, and wildlife encounters, but these are rare. The further toward the equator, the more parasitism and infectious disease; the higher and further north, the less. You folks living in the Eastern and Southern United States have to deal with a plethora of wilderness diseases. Dead animals can be a source of fleas and lice and other biting insects that can transmit diseases to your pet. Surveillance and awareness are the keys to prevention. Pay attention to your pet. Help him avoid those dangers to which he is instinctively attracted. Examine your dog thoroughly each day after he has been hiking with you. Dogs fed a raw bone a day are less likely to scavenge for dead meat than those fed only bagged kibble. Dogs who relentlessly seek out rotten meat and garbage are trying to tell you their diet is lacking. Dogs fed a raw bone a day know where the fresh, nutritious food comes from. The raw-bone-a-day dogs are nutritionally sated and satisfied, and seldom eat things that are best left uneaten. One of my veterinary practices started selling raw frozen beef, bison, and lamb bones and we went broke due to a lack of business. If more people knew that a raw bone a day keeps the veterinarian

away, there would be lot less canine veterinary strife in the world.

Conditioning

Preparing your dog for strenuous activity is vitally important in the prevention of backcountry illness and injury. Condition your pet to withstand the rigors and load-bearing expected of him *before* embarking on trips into the backcountry. If you are using packs on your dog, follow the weight guidelines carefully. Do not overload or overwork your dog. Be aware of elevation changes and the potential for altitude sickness under duress. Carefully fit the packs to your dog, and check him frequently for pack and pressure sores. Plan your hike to minimize strenuous activity when his packs are fully loaded.

Dogs, especially young and old animals, may be more sensitive and less prepared to withstand changes in outdoor environments than people. Harsh environmental conditions can bring about illness and injury, especially in dogs accustomed to living the indoor life. To prepare your dog for more strenuous outdoor activities, take him on daily outings in various weather conditions. Prevention requires anticipating the unexpected with careful conditioning and planning. Be sure to bring along your field medical kit and any specific medical supplies or medications your veterinarian prescribes. Once you have made the proper preparations, you and your best friend can relax and enjoy the emotional and physical benefits of the human-animal bond in a natural outdoor setting!

2 Secure the Scene

Your pet is injured. It is important that you stop and take a few seconds to take an overview of the situation. You cannot help your dog if you become a victim yourself. Assess the circumstances, probable causes, and situation associated with your dog's injury. Take time to determine if the danger—for example, slipping snow, falling rocks, an irritated grizzly sow or outraged moose—remains. Danger has a tendency to accelerate, at times. Observe the area carefully; make sure the commotion has not attracted another wild animal, and that no dangerous or unstable geologic condition such as a cliff, hot pool, or river lie around the corner.

Be especially careful when dealing with other animals. If your dog is fighting with a wild animal, retreat until the fight subsides. In certain rare circumstances, you may be able to use diversionary tactics to scare wildlife off, but take care. Any action other than retreat may result in the wild animal attacking you or others, including other dogs with your party, so do not draw unwarranted attention to yourself.

If there is a wildlife encounter and the wild animal who has bitten someone somehow dies, consider saving the head for a rabies check. This is critically important if the animal has somehow managed to bite you or your pet. If rabies cannot be ruled out by diagnostic testing of the suspected animal's brain, you may have to undergo prophylactic rabies immunizations.

To break up dogfights, it may sometimes be appropriate to douse the dogs with water and pull the hind legs out from the aggressive dog, but, again, be aware that any aggressive action on your part can subject you to serious attack by any animal.

CHAPTER 3

Restraint and Physical Examination

The Importance of Restraint

If you think your dog has an injury or is sick, but you are not sure what is wrong, take the precaution to comfortably observe and then restrain your pet before beginning a systematic examination. *A painful dog will bite, and she often doesn't discriminate as to who she will bite.* In treating inured dogs through the decades, I have had the opportunity to appreciate biting. The veterinary view is that if an animal—any animal—has teeth, it evolved to bite people under certain conditions. Biting is a natural defense mechanism unrelated to how your dog feels about you or others under normal circumstances. Protect yourself, calm your dog, and utilize proper restraint and a leash before examining the injury. Fear, disease, electrolyte imbalance, blood sugar fluctuations, injury, malaise, and pain can alter your beloved pet's expected stellar behavior. Avoid getting yourself or your assistants bitten, please. Maintain rabies immunity in your dog. After the initial and second vaccination, you can elect to have titers taken rather than implementing relentless vaccinations if that is your non-vaccinating preference.

Leash and Table Your Dog

If your dog is active and mobile and the injury does not appear life-threatening, give him time to calm down. Relax, and take your pulse, because in a while I am going to have you take your dog's pulse. To learn to take your own heart rate provides the basis for you to monitor your dog's heart rate.

It may be best to first observe your dog without handling. What is your heart rate? The higher your heart rate, the less likely your dog will allow you to handle her.

For best results, leash and table your dog before beginning your examination and treatment.

While you are getting your heart rate down, watch your dog's behavior; let her tell you where the injury is located. They often lick injured areas. How does she walk? You do not need to touch her to observe how she walks. Use your voice and gestures to reassure her you are there to help, rather than aggravate the pain of the injury. Leash your dog to help ensure your own safety as well as that of others. Many dogs feel reassured when leashed, or should. Some dogs run away when frightened and hurt, so a leash will help avoid that.

Take your dog out of his earthly element and into your structured plan. Move your dog into your element by carefully petting and relaxing her. If the injury allows, pick her up and place her on a table or some other similarly elevated object if you are in the boonies, atop a big rock, say. This is in contrast to examining the dog on the dirt where he would be, in most cases, more likely and able to resist examination. Veterinarians utilize exam tables because dogs seem to appreciate an examination when placed upon a table, somehow, especially injured dogs. Many dogs accept treatment in this elevated fashion, having been taken out of their element and put into your caring hands. If your dog allows close inspection and medical treatment of the injured area, no restraint other than a leash may be necessary. Pay close attention to your dog's response to treatment and respect any reluctance, whining, or nipping as requests for a more careful and patient inspection. Take time to comfort your dog. Allow him the time and space to get used to the idea that treatment may create further discomfort. Field medicine is best administered in a measured and patient fashion— it may take hours or more to reassure the dog and gain the trust needed for him to allow even an examination. Be patient—the primary rule of medicine is *First, do no harm*. Do not violate this rule. If attempts to examine and treat become unmanageable, stop and reassess the situation.

Licking and Protecting

First, do no harm.

Let me mention that I have attended to many dogs who would have been better off managing the injury by themselves, rather than becoming victim to the misguided or overzealous treatment of their guardian. Dogs are born to heal, and one must stay out of the way at times to allow healing to commence. If your dog will not allow examination or treatment, and all appears stable and the injury is not behavior-altering or life-threatening, sometimes it is best to wait and watch and head towards a veterinarian.

Licking often indicates an injury or discomfort at the site. It is not necessarily a good thing. Ten or twenty licks of a wound every hour is all a wolf is usually able to manage, and that seems about the right amount of licking to allow a wounded domestic dog. Domestic dogs often lick more than is beneficial, so one must monitor and evaluate relentless licking. Licking is often the first indication that allows you to locate an injury that is not readily visible or palpable, however excessive licking often leads to irritation of the wound, especially open wounds, punctures not so much.

Licking, especially over a period of days, often becomes obsessive-compulsive or stereotypic, so it is often wise to keep the dog preoccupied than to allow excessive licking of open wounds. Licking can be managed by covering the wound, or by providing enrichment strategies such as raw bone chewing and long measured walks if the injury allows.

The Neck-Skin Grasp

While this may not be the most comfortable experience your dog has ever had, physical restraint may at times be essential to administer pallative or life-saving measures. Preferably, your dog will have been taught that a neck-skin grasp is a good and friendly restraint method from time to time. If your dog will not allow examination on a table with a simple leash restraint, gently grasp the skin on top of his neck and bunch it firmly. This is how his mother restrained him as a youngin'. After reassuring the dog that this grasp is in his best interest, continue your exam or treatment. Grasp more firmly as more restraint is needed, to a degree. No wrestling, please. Some dogs do not allow examination, and so in certain cases an examination, not to mention treatment, may not be possible. Head to your veterinarian as the need for treatment situation indicates. You may need to lift the dog's front end off the ground or table to achieve the desired restraint effect, or the entire dog, perhaps. Remember that proper restraint is in the dog's

Caution: Some dogs, whether because of their inherent nature or the pain associated with an injury, will not allow physical restraint of any sort. In these cases, a veterinarian is essential in treating the problem.

best interest, especially if you do not have a veterinary anesthesiologist along. Veterinarians anesthetize dogs that do not allow handling to treat injuries, and that is where you may end up if your dog refuses treatment, of course.

The advantages of familiarizing your dog with physical restraint are tremendous and, in some cases, lifesaving. Fearful, skeptical, or undisciplined dogs that are unwilling to be adequately restrained to permit examination and treatment are at a distinct disadvantage. Train your dog ahead of time to allow you to examine him. All veterinarians appreciate dogs that have been trained to submit to having their paws, ears, mouth, and other anatomy examined without fear or resentment. Your pet will also be able to avoid the inconvenience, risk, and discomfort of having to be sedated or anesthetized merely to treat routine or minor injuries after he arrives at the doctor's office.

In dogs that have been previously accustomed to this method of restraint, the neck-skin grasp works well for most first aid treatments. However, the dog world is not a perfect world. If your dog violently resents restraint or examination, it may be wise to back off and allow a veterinarian to deal with the problem. Additionally, a dog's ability to avoid handling may indicate the injury

In order to properly examine your dog, you may need to use the neck-skin grasp to lift the front part of his body off the table.

is not seriously debilitating or life-threatening and that continued attempts at inspection and treatment may cause more harm than good.

The neck-skin grasp usually provides excellent restraint and can prevent a dog's ability to bite if done firmly. Grasping the nap of the neck is a crude form of acupressure that stimulates the release of endorphins, the body's natural painkillers. I cannot stress how helpful it can be to familiarize your dog with restraint as part of his training. Proper restraint is not unkind; it is a necessity that can be lifesaving.

The Half Nelson Stretch

Some injured dogs require serious restraint to preserve or restore their health. For uncooperative dogs, one of the most efficient forms of restraint is the *half nelson stretch*. As you move into this restraint, talk to your dog soothingly. Place the dog on his side (in this example, his right side) on the table with the assistance of the neck-skin grasp. "Lie down, Fido. Oh, good boy. Thank you. What a good dog." Place your forearm across the side of his upper neck and grasp the lower (right) front leg near the elbow as high up on the limb as possible. "You're okay. It's going to be all right." Pull the dog into your torso and lean into his neck with your forearm while pulling up on

the lower leg with the same hand. With your free hand, grasp his hind legs above the paws and stretch the dog. This method works only when the dog is lying fully on his side.

The half nelson stretch, when deftly and bravely applied, offers significant restraint and prevents unwanted movement while another person examines the injury and administers first aid. When applied firmly, it will minimize the dog's ability to bite, provided the position can be held. Most unhappy dogs can be successfully restrained in this manner for their own benefit. If a dog has the capacity and physical energy to resist this method, then treatment should be left to your more experienced veterinarian.

The half nelson stretch is an extremely effective method of restraint.

Muzzles

You may need a muzzle in order to treat a dog that bites. You might want to muzzle your dog before restraining him with a half nelson. The neck-skin grasp may or may not be necessary to apply the muzzle. Make a loop out of a four-foot length of conforming gauze bandage, triangular bandage or other suitable material (rope perhaps), with an overhand knot (the first part of a tying your shoelace) loosely placed at the top of the loop. From behind the dog, place the loop around his snout and draw the loop as far back as possible while tightening. Loop and then tie the ends under the jaw with another overhand knot. Then tie the remaining lengths behind the ears with a shoelace knot that can be untied quickly if necessary.

Caution: Never use muzzles on vomiting dogs or dogs in respiratory distress

If you must muzzle your dog in order to give him essential first aid, you are not unkind, you are merely doing what is necessary. You are of no use to your dog if you are sitting in the emergency room waiting to have bite punctures treated.

Properly fitting, manufactured muzzles work well, but keep in mind that no restraint is perfect. All methods must be applied patiently and carefully. Be careful—a dog can bite during all stages of restraint, examination, and treatment. Again, if your dog is healthy enough to prevent an examination despite your best efforts, then it may be wisest to transport him to a veterinarian for professional handling. Remember, *first do no harm*.

To apply a muzzle: 1. Leash dog. Tie gauze above muzzle with an overhand knot.

2. Wrap ends under muzzle and tie again.

3. Draw ends behind ears and tie a shoelace knot that can be readily loosened.

Examining Your Dog—Determining the Seriousness of Injury and Illness

If you suspect your dog has been injured or is sick, but do not know where or what is wrong—or how wrong—stop, collect your wits, leash and table the animal, and begin a systematic and thorough exam.

Gentle your dog and feel inside his mouth above the upper teeth behind the cheek. The mouth should feel wet and warm, rather than sticky and cold. Lift his upper lip to check his gums for color. Pink is good; pink is normal; pink indicates little likelihood a life-threatening situation is impending. After the gums are checked, systematically feel your dog *everywhere*. A good canine field medical responder is a thorough responder. If the right leg is injured, it may be wise to feel the left leg first to let your displacements carefully, using the opposite normal limb as a reference.

Attempt to locate the specific area of pain, injury, or discomfort. While feeling and bending the limbs, note if your dog winces, whines, or pulls away or is reluctant to allow a certain area of his body to be examined. Watch for any misshapen or unsymmetrical appearances. Take note of the presence of hair loss or blood, and try to determine its source. Once again, compare the injured body part (eye, ear, ribs, limb, footpad, etc.) to the opposite, normal body part, or to the corresponding anatomy of another dog. Spending five or ten minutes examining the normal body part will not only help you understand the extent and severity of the injury, but will help reassure your dog of your healing intentions. Significant dog-handling finesse and patience are required to effectively implement field medicine.

Vital Signs

Vital signs are the measurements of essential physiologic functions—temperature, pulse, and respiration (TPR)—as well as gum color and capillary refill. Pink gums reflect normal circulation, respiration, and heart function. Pale, white, purple, or muddy gums indicate significant injury or illness. The vital signs measured and compared sequentially over time reflect the seriousness of injury

---

Dog First Aid Tip

It will be of great benefit to both you and your dog if he is accustomed to the examination procedures as part of your routine care. He will thus be calmer and more accepting of your touch in an emergency situation when it really counts.

---

or illness and help determine how you should address the problem at hand before seeking professional care. Heartbeats per minute, breaths per minute, temperature, and gum appearance vary with your pet's breed, age, conditioning, size, diet, and state of activity. In order for you to correctly assess your dog's condition in an emergency, it is important that you are familiar with these normal vital signs before an injury or illness occurs. Write the normal values in the back cover of this book. It is essential to record and track the progression of the vital signs during an emergency. If this is done, you will always know whether the problem is getting better or worse, which is critical. The effective application of field medicine is dependent on accurate assessment.

Average Rates at Rest

Respiration—15 to 30 breaths per minute. If the dog is *not* panting, observe the chest rise and fall (one full breath). Count the breaths per minute. Panting due to heat and exercise skews the respiratory rate. Since dogs sweat only at the margins of their footpads, they pant to dissipate heat and cool themselves. Respiratory function is difficult to determine in a panting dog.

The time required for your dog to recover from panting, heat, and exercise is important. Panting should diminish within fifteen minutes after exercise in cool conditions. Persistent or excessive panting in the absence of exercise or heat can indicate pain, illness, anxiety, or injury.

Resting pulse or heart rate—50 to 150 beats per minute. The average dog's heart beats 80 times per minute. Small breeds and pups have faster and larger breeds slower resting rates. Dogs that are conditioned and in shape have lower heart rates than dogs that are not accustomed to daily running, playing, hunting, or working. There is significant variability between individual dogs. Know your dog's normal resting rate. You can feel the heartbeat low in the chest between your dog's elbows. The hind leg pulse can be felt along the

Location of the dog's heart is between the dog's front elbows.

femoral artery inside of the thigh very high in the groin along the femur (thigh bone).

Temperature—100° to 103° Fahrenheit. A thermometer gives the only accurate measure of body temperature. A dry or wet nose indicates hydration rather than temperature, although feverish dogs are vulnerable to dehydration. If a thermometer is not available, feel inside the mouth. If it is cold, shock or low body temperature are likely present. You may be able to determine if a fever is present by feeling deeply into your dog's ears with your thumbs. These will give you clues to the dog's body temperature; however, doctors want numbers, and for your pet's sake, you should, too.

An accurate temperature is taken rectally with a clean, lubricated (K-Y Jelly, Vaseline, or soap) rectal thermometer. A digital thermometer is easiest to read. There is no need to shake it down, and, unless the batteries fail, it is more dependable and less likely to break in the backcountry. Water can damage a digital thermometer, so keep it dry.

Taking the temperature rectally also gives you the opportunity to examine the rectal area and feces. If you cannot insert the thermometer, you may be able to pinpoint constipation as the cause. Pain or redness can indicate diarrhea that you did not otherwise observe. You should also note the odor of the stool and the presence of any blood on the thermometer.

Capillary refill time (CRT)—less than one second. Pink or pale pink is the normal color of unpigmented gums. Black gums cannot be used to determine capillary refill time, but somewhere in most dogs' mouths, there is some unpigmented gum tissue to use. The time it takes for capillaries to refill after they have been blanched by finger pressure determines the state of the dog's circulation, a critical parameter. The capillary refill time should be less than one and one half seconds.

You can assess the capillary refill time by applying light finger pressure on the gums above the upper

---

Normal Resting Vital Signs

Pink gums and tongue, one second capillary refill time
Heart rate—50-150 beats per minute
Respiratory rate—15-30 beats per minute
Temperature—100°-103° F

teeth, blanching the area by pushing the blood out of the capillaries. Sometimes it takes a couple of pushes, sensitizing the gums to get a better reading. After removing your finger, the whitened gum should refill to its normal pink color within one second, indicating the circulation is relatively normal and that shock or circulatory failure is not imminent.

If the gum capillaries take two seconds or longer to refill (return to color), shock may be present and veterinary care should be sought, especially if the refill time increases over time. A three-second refill time is grave. Longer refill times, or purple, discolored gums indicate big trouble. In those cases, you should stabilize the dog, provide assisted breathing and heart massage as needed, and seek immediate veterinary care.

If the weather is moderate, your healthy pet should recover to his normal parameters of respiration, heart rate, temperature, and pink gums within fifteen minutes of rest after strenuous activity. Hot weather may cause persistent panting, indicating your dog requires cooling. If your dog requires a prolonged time to recover to his normal vital signs, this indicates serious illness, heat prostration, internal injuries, or circulatory shock.

Examination Protocol

Head: systemically inspect, smell, and feel the ears, eyes, nose, mouth, teeth, tongue, oral cavity, and neck.

Legs: Check for obvious irregularities of the joints and bones; then move to the foot and check each toenail and each pad for cracks, cuts, or abrasions. Explore the webs of the feet, removing any foreign bodies such as awns or burrs.

Chest: Feel the chest movement. If labored or irregular, carefully listen with your ear placed on the chest. Determine the breaths per minute to obtain a reference value to monitor subsequent improvement or deterioration of the condition.

Abdomen: Gently palpate the tummy, a hand on each side. Note any tenderness, enlargements, or emptiness. Listen for gut sounds (borborygmi). Check the anus and reproductive organs. Observe any fecal staining and watch for future bowel movements, specifically their color and frequency. Note any distress involved performing this function. Pay attention to your dog's appetite and drinking. Note the frequency, contents, and volume of any vomiting. A bloated abdomen is an extremely serious sign and may be indicative of a life-threatening condition, especially if the bloat occurs rapidly and is accompanied by labored breathing, weakness, and discoloration of the gums.

Vital Signs: Measure and record your dog's vital signs; that is numerically determine his breathing rate, pulse, and temperature. *These are gauges that can clearly determine the seriousness of your dog's injuries.* This is the definitive field method to assess the gravity of an injury or illness. To know how seriously your dog is injured, these indices must be measured, and then periodically re-measured, in order to chart for better or worse the progression of your dog's condition.

The gums should be examined and monitored for pinkness, wetness, warmth, and capillary refill during the course of any suspected illness or injury.

A thorough inspection of the mouth is important in evaluating all injuries and illnesses.

Take advantage of light to carefully examine your dog. Eye injuries, ear problems, and mouth issues should be thoroughly explored with adequate lighting.

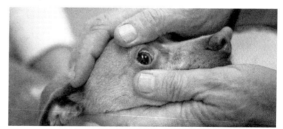

The eye should be carefully examined, and the third eyelid exposed with gentle pressure below the eye.

PART II   ADMINISTERING FIRST AID

First, do no harm

Dog Down and Out - Not Breathing - Gums Purple

1. Begin chest presses every five seconds for two minutes.
If gums do not turn pink...

If there are signs of life STAY WITH IT, repeat cycle and get to a veterinarian.

2. Begin mouth to nose breathing for two minutes. Stop and evaluate heartbeat and gums.
If no heartbeat and gums *not* pinking...

3. Begin heart massage and continue mouth to nose breathing for 10-20 minutes.

5 Dogs in Need of Emergency CPR

Cardiopulmonary resuscitation (CPR) is the simulation of vital functions. You do for your dog what he cannot do for himself—breathe and pump blood. You must compress the heart and lungs to make them perform their vital function.

Causes: Serious bodily injury.

Signs: Dog not breathing, gums purple, dog out.

Prevention: Accident avoidance. Vigilant attention to your pet and his surroundings.

Treatment: *Immediate care is necessary to save the dog's life.*

Begin measured chest presses and releases (CPR-1) every five seconds for one to two minutes. If gums do not turn pink, attempt mouth-to-nose (CPR-2) for one to two minutes. If there is still no response, perform heart massage in addition to mouth-to-nose breathing (CPR- 3).

CPR-1—Chest Presses

Push in on the chest at five-second intervals to assist breathing (contraindicated with penetrating chest wounds, broken ribs, and any other significant chest trauma).

Note: One quick chest press can clear an obstructed airway and should be done before attempting mouth-to-nose respiration.

Place your dog on his side and stimulate his inner nostrils with a cotton swab or a stem of clean, smooth grass. This may initiate a sneeze followed by breathing. If not, gently grasp and pull out his tongue, checking his mouth for foreign bodies and color. Begin chest presses to compress the lungs and simulate reflexive breathing. Slowly depress the chest for one second, release, and

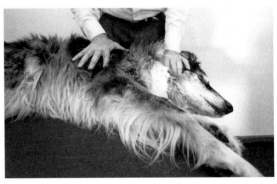

To perform chest presses, place your dog on his side and use your open hand to "breathe" the chest. Press air out and then allow air to reflexively flow back in. Repeat.

allow three or four seconds for the chest to expand and inhale air.

Repeat presses every five seconds for one to two minutes. Stop occasionally to observe if breathing has spontaneously resumed. Monitor the color of the gums and tongue. A return to pink is a sign of recovery.

Feel for the heartbeat in the lower anterior chest between the dog's elbows. If present and the gums consciousness or breathes on his own. If there is no response in two to three minutes, administer mouth-to-nose resuscitation (CPR-2).

Mouth-to-nose resuscitation will be necessary if chest presses do not revive your dog.

CPR-2—Mouth-to-Nose Resuscitation

Firmly grasp your dog's tongue and pull it out. (You can use a clean rag for traction if one is handy.) Look and explore for anything that may be lodged in the throat or mouth, obstructive or otherwise. Attempt to remove anything that might be present. With a brisk chest press (CPR-1), clear the airways. If (a) nothing is expelled and the gums remain purple, (b) no heartbeat is felt, or (c) the dog is still unconscious, begin mouth-to-nose resuscitation.

Clasp your dog's mouth with your hand and cover his nostrils with your lips. Blow in for one second, gently at first; release; after a second, push lightly on chest to assist exhalation. Repeat until gums become pink and the dog begins breathing on his own. Feel for a heartbeat;

Dog First Aid Tip

Frequently check gums for color and capillary refill to monitor the effectiveness of your CPR. If gums are becoming pinker, you are making progress. Continue assisted breathing with chest massage and mouth-to-nose resuscitation until the dog breathes on his own and the heart spontaneously beats. Continue as needed, and transport your pet to a veterinarian.

if heartbeat is present, continue until the dog is able to breathe on his own and his gums become pink. If there is no heartbeat, begin heart massage (CPR-3).

CPR-3—Heart Massage

When there is still no heartbeat and no pink gums in response to mouth-to-nose breathing, start heart massage and continue mouth-to-nose resuscitation. Squeeze the heart with your fingers placed between the dog's elbows. Use firm, repetitive one-second bursts to pump blood.

Continue mouth-to-nose resuscitation.

Use chest presses to assist exhalation of the air you have blown in. If you are alone, alternate mouth- to-nose with heart pushes, with the pattern of one forced breath, five heart pumps.

Repeat for ten minutes or until breathing and heartbeat are restored.

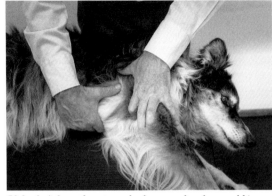

If the dog's heart has stopped, place your hand around his chest between his elbows, and massage the heart to pump blood through his body.

CHAPTER

6 Choking

Causes: Foreign object in throat, tonsillitis, throat swelling, throat trauma.

Signs: Dog awake but struggling to breathe. Something appears to be stuck in throat causing distress. It is important to differentiate blockage of the airways, a serious issue, from irritation of the throat (less serious, the dog *can* breathe).

Prevention: Prevent chewing of or play with inappropriate objects. Frequent enrichment with raw bones often fulfills certain dogs' nutritional needs, wherein they discontinue seeking unsavory things to chew and ingest. A raw bone a day keeps the veterinarian away!

Treatment: Open your dog's mouth, locate, and remove any foreign objects. Sometimes objects are stuck in or between the teeth. A tool such as a spoon or pliers may help. Understand that some foreign bodies allow normal breathing, despite the dog exerting great effort to dislodge them. A quick press to the chest with an open hand while the dog is on his side may expel the obstruction that is blocking the airflow. The gums gradually turn purple if the animal cannot breathe and turn pink when breathing is restored.

Obstructed Airway—Gums Purple

Lay your dog on his side with his head lower than the rest of his body and quickly push on the chest with an open hand. Push harder and more quickly if the first attempt fails to push air out of the nose.

Reach in his mouth and pull out his tongue. With wet fingers feel if air passes out the nostrils with each chest push. Continue gently breathing for the dog until you restore his spontaneous breathing.

If breathing is not restored and the gums remain purple, and it has been definitively determined that indeed a foreign body is blocking the airway, a tracheotomy may be necessary to allow air to reach the lungs. A tracheotomy is a dangerous medical procedure when attempted by inexperienced individuals. Improperly done with the wrong instrument, it can cause serious harm (laceration of the carotid artery). On the other hand, the dog may not be able to continue living without it.

Tracheotomy

Note: If the foreign body cannot be removed, a 14 or 16- gauge 5/8-inch needle can be used to enter the windpipe below the blockage, allowing air to pass through the needle into the airway. Make sure the trachea is immobilized between your index finger and thumb before inserting the needle. Carefully pass the needle into the trachea so air can pass in and out of the needle. Consult your veterinarian on instructions to perform this emergency veterinary surgical procedure. Keep the needle in place to allow air to pass in and out of the lungs while seeking medical care to remove the obstruction or reduce the throat swelling. Snakebites, certain stings and allergies, and trauma can cause swelling that has the potential to obstruct or block the airways. If necessary, use assisted breathing (CPR-1) after the needle is successfully inserted. To use a scalpel or knife to open the trachea is riskier than using a wide gauge needle, as many vital structures may inadvertently be lacerated.

Caution: *First do no harm.* Tracheotomies are complicated. A precise knowledge of canine anatomy and physiology is essential. If the dog can move, a tracheotomy should not be attempted.

7 Coughing

Signs: Retching, coughing, and difficulty breathing.

Causes: Kennel cough, tonsillitis, throat injuries, foreign bodies in nose or throat, irritations (skunk spray), heart disease (wet cough at rest), high altitude sickness, parasitism, allergies, infections, failure to adequately condition your dog to withstand backcountry rigors. Old age.

Prevention: Vaccination prevents distemper, kennel cough, parainfluenza, and other contagious infections acquired from association with dogs at boarding kennels, dog shows, field trials, pet shops, animal shelters, and other dog gatherings. Keep your dog away from irritating substances and plant materials.

A thorough veterinary examination before heading into the backcountry is always recommended. Avoid the use of flea, heartworm, or tick chemicals unless a definite threat is known or demonstrated, as these drugs can have serious side-effects for dogs expected to exercise extensively.

Treatment: Mouth and throat inspection often reveals the cause of the cough and can also help rule out the presence of a foreign body. Many types of coughing give the impression that something is caught in the throat. Although this is quite possible, especially in light of a history of the dog chewing or eating inappropriate objects, it often is not the case.

An irritated throat or inflamed tonsils incite the dog's coughing and retching reactions and it looks like he is trying to expel something from his throat.

Perform an airway exam. Restrain and table your dog. Open his mouth and look down the throat. Remove any foreign bodies present. Note the tonsils, normally the color of the rest of the inside of the mouth. Tonsillitis (inflammation of the tonsils) results in inflamed red strips of lymphoid tissue in the back of the throat, often indicative of an infectious disease such as kennel cough. Check under the tongue; this is often the site of a trapped fishing line or other string. Monitor and record your dog's vital signs. Note any abnormal sounds and odors. Rest your dog. Seek veterinary care if abnormalities are present or your dog is listless.

Reverse-sneezing is another syndrome that can seem quite serious with long uncomfortable sneezing spasms. It can be caused by small plant particles or other foreign bodies in the nose. The dog will violently inhale in a noisy, repetitive manner in an attempt to dislodge the irritation. Closely examine the inside of the dog's nose and remove carefully any foreign body. Sometimes the dog himself accomplishes the foreign body expulsion task with this awkward and alarming breathing maneuver.

Veterinary care and treatment are necessary if coughing, sneezing, and other respiratory issues worsen or fail to resolve. If the symptoms are accompanied by fever and malaise, discontinue exercise and see your veterinarian.

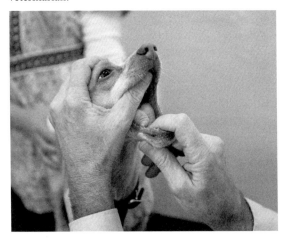

Check your dog's mouth and nose carefully for throat and tongue irritation in cases of coughing and sneezing.

High Altitude Trouble: Pulmonary Edema

Altitude Sickness

Pulmonary edema/altitude sickness can include swelling of the lungs or accumulation of fluid that interferes with effective breathing. Struggling for air is uncomfortable, and afflicted dogs cannot catch their breath.

Many dogs coming to altitude manifest symptoms of underlying heart disease that was asympotamtic at sea level. Weak hearts and lungs become even weaker at altitude. It is possible to prevent lung and heart issues with medication prescribed by your veterinarian.

Causes: Unacclimated to high altitudes accompanied by high altitude activity. Distressed, rapid, relentless, or difficult breathing may be associated with underlying medical conditions such as heart disease, respiratory infection, asthma, collapsing trachea, etc. That said, the healthiest dogs and humans can succumb to the vagaries of altitude sickness from time to time. The body likes oxygen, and when oxygenation becomes impaired, breathing troubles can be intense.

Heart weaknesses and lung conditions contribute to the severity of the condition, as can allergies and infection. Slow acclimation to altitude is recommended. Subtle conditions not apparent at lower altitudes may present themselves clinically under the duress of altitude and exercise. Aging dogs become susceptible as time wears on. Just because Fido had an uneventful climb last year doesn't mean the trip will be a merry one this year. Don't forget your dog's annual physical before tackling the mountain peaks this year.

Signs: Difficult and labored breathing caused by airway inflammation or fluid in the airways and/or lungs. Your pet tires easily and requires frequent rests, refuses to continue (can't continue); relentless panting fails to diminish with rest. The dog may refuse to sit or lie down, as those postures makes breathing more difficult. As the condition worsens, coughing and blood-tainted spittle accompanies shortness of breath. Milder cases of altitude sickness manifest as coughing at night, often beginning a few hours after activity has subsided. The dog may prefer a sitting position with the elbows held wide and head stretched out, refusing to lie down. Other signs include a worried expression, distressed eyes and unremitting panting.

In young dogs, the cause can be congenital heart disease or anemia from internal parasites. Older or heavy dogs may suffer from congestive heart failure. Backup of fluid into the lungs from a weak or aging heart is aggravated by strenuous or even mild activity at high elevations. Intake of untoward amounts of salt can aggravate heart disease and pulmonary edema. Many aging dogs should be on a low sodium, or sodium-free diet.

Prevention: Careful conditioning and *gradual* acclimation to high altitudes is recommended before all high altitude trips. Proper medical treatment of underlying health conditions can prevent exercise-associated breathing complications at any altitude. Avoid strenuous exercise—especially at high altitudes—to which your dog is not accustomed, difficult snow (deep, wind-pressed, crusted) and extremes of hot or cold weather. See your veterinarian for a physical exam and consultation prior to departure. He or she will discuss proper conditioning and consider the need for administration of preventive and ameliorative medications, which can be critical as this condition is life-threatening. Avoid salt, and salty treats, bacon, ham, and cheap dog treats.

Treatment: Discontinue activity. Transport the dog to a lower altitude in a manner that allows easy breathing. If the gums become pale or purple, mouth-to-nose breathing may be necessary until the gums regain their normal color and refill time. Administer oxygen if available, which it often is at high altitudes. I recommend that you bring it for yourself and your dog if you plan to travel at elevations where there could be problems. Simply allow the oxygen to flow near your dog's nostrils, rather than into the mouth, in a wind-free environment.

Seek veterinary care if breathing difficulty doesn't improve with rest or the return to a lower elevation. Subsequent or underlying lung disorders or infections and aggravation of pre-existing medical conditions can complicate altitude sickness. See your veterinarian if your dog experiences difficulty breathing or tires easily on high altitude hikes. Furosemide is a commonly employed pharmaceutical treatment. It is a diuretic which lowers the arterial blood pressure in the lungs. Side effects include electrolyte imbalances and dehydration.

9 Near Drowning

Causes: Waterborn in fast-moving water conditions that exceed your dog's swimming abilities.

Signs: Struggling to swim or emerge from fast-flowing waters. Unconsciousness in or near water.

Prevention: Keep your dog away from fast-moving, high-banked, or flooding rivers, regardless of your confidence in the dog's ability to swim. Most drownings occur in water dogs. Make sure your dog is well rested before swimming. Do not encourage strenuous swimming at high altitudes or in fast-flowing streams, and consider the degree of your dog's cumulative exhaustion.

Treatment: Get the water out of the lungs, restore normal breathing and heartbeat.

Hold the dog upside down, suspended by his hind legs, and allow any water to drain out of the airways while an assistant firmly but slowly squeezes the chest. This may need to be repeated.

Place the dog with his head and chest sloping downhill and use chest presses and heart massage as needed to restore breathing and heartbeat. Withhold mouth-to-nose resuscitation until most of the water has been expelled from the lungs or the dog's condition appears gravely critical. (Mouth-to-nose may blow airway water deeper into the lungs or prevent its expellation.)

Use chest presses to expel water from your dog's lungs as he lies with head and chest sloping downhill.

10 Coma

Causes: Pre-existing medical conditions including endocrine disease and vital organ failures, head injuries, trauma, stroke, heat prostration, gastric torsion, overwhelming infection, dehydration, electrolyte imbalance, hypoglycemia, hypothermia, circulatory collapse, heart attack, and others.

Signs: Dog down and unaware of his surroundings. No blink elicited when the skin above or below the eyelids touched. Dog unconscious.

Prevention: Regular veterinary exams, blood tests, and consultations.

Treatment: Open the dog's mouth and check the airway. Check his breathing and gums. Keep his head lower than the rest of his body to avoid aspiration (inhalation of fluids or objects). If the dog has stopped breathing and has purple gums, administer CPR.

Check the eyes, noting the size of the pupils. Cover the eyes for three minutes and the observe pupillary constriction in response to daylight. Use a flashlight if it is dark. Avoid direct sunlight. The desired pupillary response is that the pupil constricts (gets smaller) in response to light. Fixed and dilated pupils that do not respond to light indicate a grave state. Seek veterinary care immediately.

Warm the dog up if a low body temperature is associated with the unconsciousness.

Rub small amounts of sugar or honey onto the gums every fifteen minutes if hypoglycemia or insulin shock is suspected.

Cool the dog down with luke-cool water for heatstroke.

In case of traumatic injuries, stabilize your dog for immediate transport to veterinary care when his breathing and heartbeat become stable.

Dog First Aid Tip

It is important to differentiate coma from paralysis. With paralysis, the dog is conscious, aware of you and his surroundings, and his pupils are usually responsive to light. Possible causes of paralysis include spinal injury, electrolyte imbalance, and tick bites. Stabilize the animal and transport him to veterinary care for diagnosis and treatment.

CHAPTER 11 Shock—Circulatory Collapse

Causes: Severe injury, internal or external blood loss, overwhelming pain, fear, dehydration, or altitude sickness (pulmonary edema, swollen lungs). Burns, infection, twisted gut or stomach, snakebites, drug or allergic reactions, or poisoning can also cause circulatory failure.

Prevention: Awareness of any underlying medical conditions and being appropriately prepared for exercise in extreme conditions and adverse environments.

Mild Shock

Signs: Weak dog with shallow or labored breathing, pale or muddy gums.

Treatment: Rest your dog. Many cases of mild shock respond to rest. If mild shock worsens despite rest and the vital signs deteriorate, it is a sign of serious underlying troubles. Cease all activity and comfort your dog. A full body massage may reveal the source of problem. Make provisions for warmth and encourage fluid intake. Allow his body to recover normal breathing and circulatory status. Monitor his breathing rate, pulse, and gums.

Severe Shock

Signs: Dog unable to walk, unable to move, comatose, muddy or purple gums. As shock progresses, the dog becomes weak and woozy.

Monitor capillary refill time by pressing the gums above the teeth with your finger. Release and count the seconds required for color (pinkness) to return, normally one second. Longer refill times indicate that the vessels and heart are not adequately circulating the blood, and/or that the lungs may be damaged (perhaps a result of a sucking chest wound or fluid or blood in lungs).

As the circulatory failure becomes life-threatening, the body shifts blood to the vital organs. The peripheral (body surface) circulation becomes weak the animal becomes cold, his heartbeat quickens, and the pulse becomes life-threatening, the body shifts blood to the vital organs. The peripheral (body surface) circulation becomes weak, the animal becomes cold, his heartbeat quickens, and the pulse becomes thready (barely detectable). If the resting heart rate surpasses 150 beats per minute, serious trouble is at hand.

Treatment: Comfort, stabilize, and transport the dog to veterinary care for therapy—catheterization, IV fluids and glucocorticoid administration—and a diagnostic workup.

Provide oxygen if available. Control external bleeding with direct pressure.

NONRESPONSIVE

Shock Due to Allergic Reactions (Anaphylactic Shock)

Prevention: Avoid unnecessary drug administration; minimize exposure to stinging insects and pollens that are known to be offensive to your pet or pets in general. Avoid poison ivy, stinging nettles, house-plants, and other species of irritating plants. Keep your pet from eating or licking harmful chemicals or other inappropriate substances.

Signs: Insect stings or bites, drug reactions, and synthetic or naturally occurring allergens can cause swelling of the face or limbs.

Treatment: Anaphylactic shock may lead to lung swelling and cardiovascular collapse. Transport your pet to his doctor. Antihistamines or cortisone may be administered as prescribed and directed by your veterinarian. Subcutaneous and intravenous fluids are often indicated, and can be lifesaving. Administer 100 ml of Lactated Ringers under the skin for every 10 pounds every four hours as the fluids are absorbed.

Caution: Do not use antihistamines to treat snake bites.

12 Seizures

Seizures are episodes of involuntary spastic activity and subconscious convulsions accompanied by varying degrees of unconsciousness. They vary by cause, type, frequency, and intensity. Minor (petit mal) seizures are subtle. The dog appears spaced-out and confused, perhaps with a loss of balance or a failure to recognize familiar people or places. These early (prodromal) signs can progress to unconsciousness and full-blown body spasms. Pressure over the eyelids on the eyeballs causes a vagal response, which may diminish or prevent seizure activity if applied during the prodromal stage. Some seizures disappear never to be noted again; others are unrelenting. A veterinary consultation should be arranged if your dog has experienced a seizure. Many outdoor seizures are isolated incidents caused by electrolyte imbalance and dehydration, sometimes more prevalent at altitude or hot days. Hydration and pre-hydration strategies minimize seizure/paralysis episodes of the electrolyte imbalance type. Labrador dogs seem prone to dehydration and subsequent neurological dysfunction. Again, gradual acclimation to perform expected activities is essential to minimize troubles of all sorts. It is the unprepared, unconditioned dog that most often becomes afflicted in the backcountry.

Causes: Epilepsy, electrolyte imbalance, poisoning (strychnine, antifreeze, mushrooms, illicit drugs, chocolate), brain infections, head injuries, prolonged fever, and canine distemper (puppies). Dehydration or heat stroke and subsequent electrolyte and blood sugar imbalances cause seizures, especially in puppies, fat dogs, and older dogs subjected to unaccustomed rigorous activity and high temperatures.

Signs: Dog behaves abnormally and becomes confused. Ataxia. Vertigo. Inability to recognize familiar people and places. Body twitches, spasms, and loss of function.

Prevention: Regular checkups, proper conditioning, and poison avoidance.

Treatment: If you recognize a seizure coming on, what is known as the pre-seizure aura, you can attempt the vagal maneuver by folding the eyelids over the eyes and applying gentle pressure to the bulbs of the eyes with your thumbs. Your fingers support the dog's jaw.

Some dogs will begin to shake, get a worried, confused, or faraway look in their eyes and exhibit an unusual demeanor before a seizure begins. It is often best to avoid attempting to control a grand mal seizure with physical restraint. Attempts to do so may worsen the spell or injure the dog or human. Instead, pad the

NONRESPONSIVE

area around the dog. Stay clear to avoid getting bitten and let the seizure pass. Avoid stimuli such as sound, touch, or restraint. If possible, note the duration of the seizure. Keep other dogs away, since some dogs, feeling threatened, will attack a dog having a seizure.

After the seizure has subsided, comfort the dog. Do not offer food or liquids for at least an hour after the seizure has ended. Apply eyeball pressure as described above for two minutes every half hour. If the dog is a known epileptic, administer the seizure medication as directed by your veterinarian.

If dehydration, hypoglycemia, or electrolyte imbalance are suspected, encourage your dog to drink an electrolyte/carbohydrate remedy (Gatorade, Pedialyte), or add a pinch of salt (low-sodium salt with potassium is best), a pinch of baking soda, and a teaspoon of sugar or honey to a pint of water. Dribble the solution into the dog's mouth after she has recovered from the seizure and is conscious, knowing, and able and willing to swallow.

Dog First Aid Tip

Keep the dog quiet. Avoid bright light, exercise, or sudden noises.

Seek veterinary care if the seizures do not stop or recur. Use a blanket to transport a dog having seizures. Wrap the dog in a blanket, restraining his limbs, lift and carry the dog. Veterinary treatment may include administration or intravenous anti-seizure drugs, diazepam and barbiturates, as well as intravenous fluids, dextrose, and electrolytes.

SECTION C: WOUNDS, BLEEDING, FRACTURES, AND CHEST INJURIES
Wounds and Bleeding

Wound Precautions

Employ cleanliness and hygienic medical techniques using washed or gloved hands when treating wounds. Flush wounds with sterile eye wash or any clean, potable water. Flush them using an irrigation syringe if contamination with infective material is obvious or suspected. Wash and rewash your hands. Use latex gloves if available. Clipping the hair may or may not be appropriate, as much of the clipped hair subsequently becomes embedded in the wound when and if the wound is stapled or closed. If the hair can be removed without contaminating the wound, fine. Sometimes the hair can be tied and utilized to close the wound in certain long-haired breeds. Sometimes dried blood holds the hair together, effectively closing the wound.

Dog First Aid Tip

Remember to properly restrain your dog with at least a leash before attempting to control bleeding. You must control the dog before you can control the bleeding.

Dogs do not have any more inherent resistance to infection than people, so be as clean as you can. Do not use strong iodine or hydrogen peroxide in open wounds, since these may damage tissue. The isotonic sterile eye wash allows a stream of rinse to be directed at the wound to flush out any debris or damaged tissue. For infected wounds it is preferred the flush be with a solution of properly diluted disinfectant. One ounce chlorhexidine in one quart of clean or treated water is the usual veterinary choice. Diluting chlorhexidine is non-irritating and extremely effective in preventing and treating infections in dogs. If the wound appears to need stitching or if it is gaping, wrapping it may serve to protect it after flushing until suturing or stapling can be achieved.

Bite wounds are the wounds most likely to develop complications due to the infective nature of an animal bite, as well as the possibility of rabies transmission. The initial bleeding of an injury serves to flush the wound from the inside out, so some bleeding is desirable to initiate the healing process. Puncture wounds that do not have a gaping nature should be thoroughly flushed, milked, explored, medicated with gentle topical antibiotics, and allowed to drain.

INJURIES

Licking

Pay attention to your dog's licking habits, please. Licking is often the first sign that an injury has been incurred, or an issue is accelerating.

A few licks have a purpose in wound debridement and cleaning. However, too much wound licking is abrasive and delays healing. If licking or biting at an injury becomes excessive or unremitting, the wound will fare much better if it is wrapped or covered. Neck collars that prevent the dog from reaching the wound can be fashioned from towels, milk cartons, or raincoats. You can also apply soap or bitter substances around wounds to discourage licking. (Of course, obedient dogs—such as those belonging to veterinarians—do not lick when told not to.)

Again, licking is often the first indication your dog has a cut or injury. The injuries do not have to be cuts or abrasions, they can be internal. Licking of the carpal joint may indicate acute carpal arthritis. Licking of the anus may indicate anal gland dysfunction, a base-of-tail injury, diarrhea, or constipation.

Bleeding/QuikClot® Gauze

Bleeding can be from arteries, veins, or capillaries. Arterial bleeding spurts rhythmically with the heartbeat and is bright red. It is more serious than venous bleeding, which is slower flowing, darker red, and seeping rather than squirting. Capillary bleeding oozes even more slowly. Not all bleeding is undesirable; if not excessive, bleeding has a purpose in flushing the wound and delivering natural immunity to the injured area. In all cases of bleeding, calm your dog as best you can in order to lower his blood pressure.

If bleeding is profuse, pulsing, or clearly life-threatening, calm and restrain your dog, and place the QuikClot® Gauze or other sterile dressing over the entire bleeding area and apply continuous *direct pressure*. Applying finger pressure to the arterial blood supply *above* the wound will minimize blood flow to the injury and aid the effectiveness of the hemorrhage control gauze.

After the bleeding stops, leave the QuikClot® Gauze or dressings and carefully wrap the dressing in place. If the bleeding is arterial and direct QuikClot® Gauze pressure does not slow the flow, encircle the limb with your hand above the bleeding while continuing the direct pressure at the source of the bleeding. Wrapping the limb may allow enough pressure to be applied on a continuous basis to stop the bleeding, especially if the dog is resentful or painful. Wrap from the paw up. If bleeding was profuse and the injury massive, please leave the wrap in place until veterinary assistance can be obtained. Let the veterinarian remove the QuikClot® gauze to treat the wound in a controlled setting, please. If wraps must be left on contaminated wound, antibiotic therapy may be instituted upon the advice and consent of your prescribing veterinarian.

Tourniquets are a last resort to stop bleeding where it obvious the limb will have to be amputated.

Nosebleeds

For nosebleeds, which are often from external trauma, rest the dog and apply ice wrapped in a washcloth to the nose and forehead. Inspect the inside of the mouth for broken teeth or other associated injuries caused by the trauma that created the nosebleed. Assess the dogs respiratory, heart, gum, and cardiac status, please. Suspect rodent poison toxicity for all unusual bleeding.

Once a wound has stopped bleeding, do not rub or wipe it unnecessarily, and minimize activity and anxiety in your dog to prevent recurrence.

If the injury is obviously contaminated, or the object that caused the wound is known to be contaminated with such things as feces or dirt, flush the area with sterile solution or disinfected water. Flush again. Gently squirt solution into the wound to dislodge obvious contaminants. Avoid water pressure that drives infective material deeper into the wound.

You can gently swab the wound with gauze dipped in clean, potable water if simple flushing does not successfully remove all debris or contaminants.

First, do no harm. Application of medicines to wounds is overrated, and can cause more harm than good by interfering with natural healing processes and creating unnecessary irritation. Curb your desire to doctor wounds with medicine and concentrate on getting the site clean and keeping it protected and clean.

Disinfected tweezers, utility tools, or hemostats can be used to remove small slivers, pieces of gravel, and

Dog First Aid Tip

Clipping the hair around a wound may result in hair getting into the injury site. Use your best judgment regarding whether to clip or cut hair to facilitate your cleaning and treatment of the wound. It may be best to leave hair unclipped. This has the added advantage of giving you the option of weaving or taping the hair as an aid in closing the wound.

INJURIES

other infective debris. Consider the possibility of broken, hidden foreign bodies in deep or extensive wounds. Flushing contaminated wounds that do not enter the thorax or abdomen is encouraged.

If necessary, wrap gaping wounds to prevent continued bleeding, avoid further contamination, provide support, and prevent excessive licking. Puncture and bite wounds may best be left uncovered to allow essential drainage. Bite wounds have a higher potential to become infected than wounds caused by inanimate objects. Burns and friction trauma that cause extensive tissue damage can be quite serious.

When choosing to wrap or cover wounds, the dog should maintain feeling below the wrap if feeling was present before its application. The limb below the wrap should remain warm to touch and sensation and should not swell. Replace a tight wrap with a looser wrap if circulation beyond the wrap appears diminished. When a wrap is changed or loosened, the sterile gauze covering the wound may be left in place so as not to start the bleeding up again, especially if the QuikClot® Gauze is in place after having successfully stopped significant bleeding.

Caution: Do not *automatically* remove large or deeply impaled foreign objects, especially those that enter the chest, abdomen, or eye. Removal can cause life-threatening bleeding, evisceration, loss of sight, or other internal disruptions that are best handled by a veterinarian in a medical facility. Use careful consideration and medical judgment when removing impaled objects. When in doubt, leave the object in place and transport the pet as carefully as possible to a veterinarian. In some cases, part of the object may be cut off to lessen additional trauma and facilitate transport of the dog. Leave enough to allow the doctor to remove the object after he has assessed the injury and stabilized the animal.

Flushing

Flush all bite wounds thoroughly. Treated or safe drinking water is often clean enough to allow superficial wound cleansing if sterile solutions are not available. Uncontaminated, clean wounds may be best left unflushed, especially if bleeding has cleared the wound of contaminants. In obviously dirty or bite- contaminated wounds, rinse the wound thoroughly with many flushings. You may need to immerse severely contaminated or bite wounds in clean running spring water if no other source of flushing solution is available; however, it is best to flush deep body wounds or punctures with sterile solutions. In areas where clean water is not available, boiled (but cooled) water or treated drinking water may have to suffice. Only specially prepared sterile eye wash solutions should be used on or near the eyes. Eye flushing solutions can also be used to clean other wounds as well.

Dog First Aid Tip

All flushing should be thorough, yet gentle. High pressure flushing is best left to a veterinarian, and whether he or she determines it necessary and appropriate. *First do no harm.*

Wraps and Bandages

Wrap gaping wounds to prevent subsequent contamination. Wraps stabilize the injury, control bleeding, and keep it clean. Once again, you need to adequately restrain your dog, and he must not fight the process. Apply wraps carefully and not too tightly. A wrap that is too tight can prevent adequate blood flow to the end of the limb, resulting in a serious loss of circulation and subsequent, sometimes irreversible, tissue damage. It is a good idea to change the initial wrap after the bleeding has completely stopped (after an hour or so) in order to reassess the injury and allow blood to flow freely to the end of the leg.

The danger of too tight a wrap can be minimized by the use of gauze wrap and cotton padding under the tighter elastic material (Vetrap, Elastikon, Cohesive Wrap) is applied. Subsequent swelling below the cohesive wrap indicates the wrap is too tight and should be immediately removed. A lack of swelling, however, does not necessarily mean that the wrap is all right. If you have any doubt about whether or not a wrap is too tight, remove or change the wrap rather than leave it on.

INJURIES

When wrapping the foot, place cotton between the toes.

Wound Closure Surgical Staple Guns

Surgical staple guns, surgical glue, wraps, and suture material can be used to close wounds. The dog must be adequately restrained, as wound closure can be painful. For many field wounds, staple guns are the most practical method to quickly close a wound, although in the long run, they may not provide adequate closure strength like mattress sutures can.

Before closure is attempted by any method, flush the wound, please, especially if the cause of the wound appears to be contaminated. Adequate flushing with sterile or potable clean water cannot be overemphasized. If wounds are to be closed, make sure infective material and contaminants are not closed inside the tissue.

After the wound is cleaned and your hands are washed or gloved, determine if the edges of the wound can be easily opposed while the dog is comfortably restrained. With the thumb and forefinger of your free hand oppose the wound margins, making sure both sides match up reasonably well. Sequentially staple the wound together. Smaller wounds should be closed top to bottom, while longer wounds may require some staples in the middle

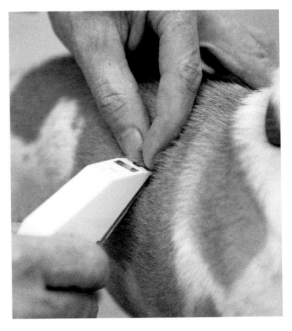

To use the skin stapler, carefully oppose the edges of the wound with your thumb and forefinger, and with light pressure insert the staple.

before suturing the margins. Some wounds become naturally numb shortly after they are incurred, and a quick stapling can at times be accomplished relatively pain free. If the object inflicting the wound was clean, and brief flush and a quick staple or two done quickly may be all that is required.

If the dog resents stapling, Cetacaine or a similar topical anesthetic can be applied to numb the wound. More effectively in trained hands, the wound margins can be injected with lidocaine if available. Once the wound is numb, the staples can be applied. Staples best serve to close wounds that do not have a lot of tension or movement. Skin staples do not hold all wounds together. In cases of significant tension, or areas of skin loss, suturing with ligatures may be preferred. Make sure the wound closure treatment does not cause more stress and pain than necessary. Dogs have a tremendous capacity to walk off and heal certain wounds, and some are best left alone depending on what the dog has to say about treatment of the wound.

Often it is not critical to have non-bleeding, superficial wounds sutured or closed immediately, although it is nice. Some dogs do not allow wounds to be closed, and for them, all other things within normal limits, it may be best to let a veterinarian manage the injury a day or two

later. First, do no harm.

It is critical is to keep open wounds clean and to prevent the dog from licking and further abrading the injury. Once again, many superficial wounds can be successfully sutured a day or two after they are incurred if veterinary care is not immediately available and the wound does not involve critical structures or invade body cavities. Degrees of swelling, pain, redness, and loss of function reflect the severity and progress of healing wounds. If a fever is present, infection is likely, and antibiotics may be in order.

Caution: It is best to leave contaminated and infected wounds open. Punctures or wounds with small openings should not be closed.

INJURIES

14 Head and Spinal Injuries

Severe Head Injury

Causes: Head trauma of many sorts.

Signs: Head contusions and lacerations, bleeding from the mouth, unconsciousness, disorientation, or broken bones, jaws, or teeth. Check the gums for pinkness. Check the dog's bite for normal alignment of the teeth. Palpate for broken bones or loose teeth. Check the pupillary response to motion and light. If the pupils are fixed, dilated, different sizes, or the dog is unable to see, the injury requires prompt veterinary attention.

Prevention: Vigilance regarding potential dangers.

Treatment: Chest massage and mouth-to-nose resuscitation will help oxygenate the brain and may need to be continuously administered until medical treatment can be obtained. Control significant bleeding with sterile, direct pressure utilizing the QuikClot® Gauze or other gauze.

Avoid pressure on the dog's throat, which could interfere with breathing or circulation. Keep his head lower than the rest of his body to allow adequate drainage of blood and saliva and to keep them from running into the lungs. A light muzzle may be applied to stabilize a broken jaw. If the eye is involved, flush it with eyewash, cover with sterile gauze, and carefully wrap.

Paralysis; Fractures of the Spine

Causes: Major trauma, hit by car, brutal falls, kicks and stomps by wildlife or horses. Poisoning.

Signs: Paralysis. Dog cannot move hind limbs. Obvious structural deformity to the neck or spine. Loss of bowel and urinary control. Partial paralysis; dog cannot use or feel his hind legs, the front legs may be rigid and the neck arched upwards. Differentiate from seizures by level of consciousness. Mushroom poisoning can cause ataxia and paralysis.

Paralysis in a conscious dog is determined by loss of use and loss of feeling in the extremities. The tail may be limp and lifeless. Touch or gently pinch the toes or webbing to elicit a withdrawal reflex in each limb. When a withdrawal response is absent, paralysis may be present, indicating central nervous system spinal nerve involvement. Stabilize the dog and spine on a board or with a sling and transport the patient to veterinary care.

Prevention: Knowledge and respect of unfamiliar or dangerous environments and conditions. Keep your dog fulfilled and enriched with raw bones and fresh meat so you dog is nutritionally sated, and avoids eating untoward things such as wild mushrooms and rotting offal.

Treatment: Stabilize and calm the dog. Note the level

of awareness and pupils of the eyes. Gently feel down his spine and note any discrepancies in the skeletal structure. When possible, secure the dog to a rigid surface with sheets or a blanket to stabilize his full length and torso width. If no board is available, you can wrap your dog in a blanket and transport him to the veterinarian. If the dog will not allow himself to be secured to a rigid structure, it may be necessary to suspend him in a blanket to transport him.

A blanket sling may take many different forms, depending on the slinging materials available.

Mouth-to-nose resuscitation will help oxygenate the brain and may need to be continuously administered until medical treatment can be obtained. Chest presses may be contraindicated as they may cause further spinal trauma if the thoracic spine is damaged.

Broken Pelvis

Causes: Any major accident involving the dog's hind end, including falling out of moving vehicles, being hit by a car, or falling long distances.

Signs: Difficulty or refusal to rise and walk. Inability to move one or both hind legs may indicate pelvic, femur, or hip injuries, often associated with severe pain. Dog may carry a hind limb or have awkward or crooked gait. Unlike spinal paralysis, there is usually a toe-pinch response if the nerves to the leg are not damaged.

Prevention: Avoid allowing pets to ride unrestrained in the back of pickup trucks.

Treatment: Restrict movement to avoid further injury. The dog may need support of his hind end to assist with defecation and urination. Allow the dog to assume the position most comfortable for him. Use a blanket sling to transport the dog in his preferred stance to a veterinarian.

INJURIES

15 Chest Wounds

External Chest Wounds

Causes: Stick punctures, gunshot. Running dog encounters a stick, barbed wire fence, or other sharp object that impales the thorax.

Signs: Chest punctures, broken ribs, objects impaling the chest, coughing up blood or foam, difficulty breathing. A sucking sound associated with breathing is cause for serious concern. Dogs attempting to lick their chest or ribs are often indicating an issue in the pectoral or thoracic area.

Prevention: Avoid reckless running over terrain with excessive downfall or other penetrating threats. Keep your dog away from livestock and off private property where he might be considered unwelcome to avoid gunshot injuries. Laws vary from state to state, but dogs that livestock owners perceive as an uncontrolled threat are sometimes shot. Likewise, certain hunters perceive untethered dogs a threat.

Treatment: *Cleanliness and sterile technique is critical when dealing with penetrating chest wounds.* Calm the dog and attempt to close the wound with sterile gauze and hand pressure. The QuikClot® Gauze can effectively seal a chest wound, but when possible, attempt to cleanse the area first. An antibiotic powder or ointment can be applied before closure of the chest wound is attempted. If bleeding is not evident or profuse, attempt to slide the surrounding intact skin over the opening and hold it in place. Stapling the skin may seal the open chest wound. Wrapping the chest may or may not be appropriate depending on the integrity of the spine and ribcage. Make sure wrap is not so tight that it limits or impairs breathing.

Monitor vital signs for breathing emergencies. The presence of chest wounds in the unconscious dog may warrant the application of mouth-to-nose resuscitation rather than chest massage. Shock often follows chest injuries. Monitor vital signs carefully, and treat the dog for shock if vital signs deteriorate. Keep the dog warm. Attempt to encourage drinking or licking of a nutritious gruel. Administer subcutaneous fluids if they have been made available by your veterinarian for such emergencies.

Internal Problems

Causes: External trauma such as falls, kicks, car accidents, and similar violent mishaps that bruise or burst the lungs. Abdominal distention, gastric torsion, and other intestinal dysfunctions of varying sorts. Internal infections are accompanied by fever. Any number of subclinical pre-existing conditions can be exacerbated by outdoor travel.

Signs: Painful and labored breathing. Exercise intolerance. Possibly internal bleeding. Altitude sickness. Anxiety caused by the shortness of breath. When the problem is serious, vital signs deteriorate. Pulse and rate of respiration increase, gums grow pale or, worse, become purple. Temperature may rise, and then drop. Be aware of even subtle changes in your dog during backcountry excursions. When things do not seem right, stop and evaluate the dog. Check the pulse, temperature, and gums. Feel the limbs, feet, and abdomen. Use a full body massage to check out all the moving parts, joints, and muscles.

Prevention: Know your dog, and know her limitations, acclimations, and realize time changes us all. Do not expose your dog to activities she has not become gradually and fully acclimated to, a tall order, I know, but one that best serves the dog.

Treatment: Calm your dog. Provide warmth and comfort and fluids. Avoid chest presses, but provide mouth-to-nose resuscitation as needed to maintain oxygenation. Return to a lower elevation. Administer subcutaneous isotonic fluids, 200 ml at a time. As the fluids become absorbed, repeat every hour.

Caution: Do not remove objects impaled deeply in the chest. Try to close the surrounding entry wound. Trim and stabilize the object. Stabilize the dog. Administer mouth-to-nose respiration as needed. Do not use chest presses. Seek veterinary care immediately, keeping the dog stabilized as best you can during transport.

INJURIES

CHAPTER 16 Lameness

The most common cause of lameness in a healthy outdoor dog is an injury to the foot. Carefully examine the nails, webs, and pads of your dog's feet when limping first appears with no other obvious cause. Move up each limb. Vulnerable joints on the front limb are the toe, carpus, elbow, and shoulder joints. Each should be flexed and felt for tenderness and swelling. Check the neck and back, and then move to the hind feet, and move up the limb. The stifle and hip joints are most often the problem. Sudden leg-carrying lamenesses require prompt investigation.

Foot Injuries

Pad, Toe, and Web Cuts

Causes: Imbedded glass, cuts inflicted by sharp objects, crushing injuries, loose river rocks, tender under-conditioned feet, overgrown or brittle toenails.

Signs: Sudden onset of limping, sometimes preceded by a yelp in rough going. Dog often repeatedly stops his activity to lick or bite at a foot. Bloody footprints are sometimes the first indication of an injury.

Cuts or lacerations of the pads or toe webbing are common. Some bleed profusely. Cut pads gape open after a period of time and can appear unsightly with a bulging, meaty appearance. They are difficult to suture if they are long standing, and difficult otherwise due to the sensitive nature of the pads.

Prevention: Proper conditioning, avoid exercise in areas where trauma is likely.

Treatment: Cleaning and wrapping (with cotton between the toes) controls bleeding and prevents further trauma and infection. Stapling can be effective if done shortly after a pad laceration is incurred, but once the laceration swells staples become counterproductive. Cold water rinses clean the area and offer pain relief. Standing in a clean mountain stream can be helpful to cleanse and numb the injury allowing treatment. QuikClot® Gauze can be applied with direct pressure and wrapped to control profuse pad bleeding.

Booties can be improvised from stockings or wrapping materials. If continued travel is to be expected, the paw injury often needs to be covered and protected. Be careful to avoid cutting off the circulation when fastening and securing booties or wraps. Moisture and motion can cause booties to tighten, resulting in loss of circulation to the injured digits. For feet tender from overexercise in rough-going situations, rest your dog when possible, and minimize further travel. Surgical glue (Nexaband) can be applied to tender pads to provide durable protection.

Toenail Injuries

Causes: Overgrown toenails, brittle toenails, rocky travel, bad luck, nailbed inflammation and infection.

Signs: Limping. Licking. Close exam reveals broken or cracked nails, which sometimes bleed, and often become painful.

Prevention: Regular exercise to wear down nails naturally while toughening them up. Periodic nail clipping, when necessary.

Treatment: Clip off the broken nail or peel the broken portion away. Clean the nail and wrap the foot.

Caution: Neither silver nitrate nor hydrogen peroxide should be used to treat large, open, bleeding, or penetrating wounds. Reserve their use to toenail injures and bleeding at the tips of the ears (which can sometimes be profuse and unremitting from repeated head shaking). Keep silver nitrate sticks away from the eyes and out of the ear canals.

If the other nails are excessively long, clip them. For nails that continue to bleed, cauterize the bleeding with silver nitrate sticks. (This may be quite painful; hydrogen peroxide is less irritating, but also less effective.) Hold off the blood supply above the toe and gently roll the silver nitrate stick on the area that has exposed vessels. Hydrogen peroxide-soaked gauze can be held on the injury to stop less profuse bleeding. Blood stop (QuikClot®) powders work well to stop nail bleeding.

Blistered Pads

Causes: Dogs inadequately conditioned for extensive foot travel, dogs packed too heavily or exercised too long over rough terrain. Foot burns from fires, hot stoves, or cookware.

Signs: Limping after unaccustomed exercise over rough terrain.

Prevention: Gradual conditioning toughens pads, making them resistant to wear-and-tear injuries while conditioning the dog. Properly fitted booties or wraps protect injured feet, and can also be used preventively. Do not overburden dogs with excessive weight if they are expected to carry packs. Applying certain substances to the feet, such as Preparation H, surgical glue, and formaldehyde, is seldom adequately effective

INJURIES

in toughening pads up. Proper conditioning is the preferred method, as it also conditions the muscles and cardiovascular system, and it avoids the possibility of the dog licking off preparations that can be toxic, upsetting to the stomach, and irritating to the mouth and tongue.

Treatment: Clean the affected pads, removing any attached or penetrating materials. Soak the paws in water with Epsom salts (a handful of salts to one quart water) or, if feasible, stand the dog in a cold stream to relieve the pain and swelling. Wrap the affected feet for protection if further travel is necessary (discontinuing exercise is preferred). Surgical glue (Nexaband) can be applied lightly to abraded, cut, or worn-through pads allowing it to dry before further exercise. The glue forms a protective coating but has its limitations. Vulnerable, foot-sore dogs should be taken to a veterinarian beforehand to obtain advice regarding care and prevention. Serious burns require immediate veterinary care.

Dewclaw Rips and Tears

The dewclaw, when present, is located on the inside of the lower leg. Some dewclaws are snug to the leg, while others are loose and poorly connected. Loose-fitting dewclaws are vulnerable to snagging and tearing injuries.

Dewclaws are vestigial toes, corresponding to human thumbs.

Signs: Limping, licking, swelling and bleeding.

Prevention: Keep dewclaw nails trimmed, as they are not worn with regular exercise.

Treatment: Clean, disinfect, and wrap the area of the limb above and below the dewclaw. Most dogs can travel adequately with this treatment. The injury is often more painful and bothersome than structurally harmful to the dog. Carrying the affected limb prevents further harm and injury. If your dog is carrying a limb, accept this protective mechanism and head to the doctor.

Some dewclaw injuries develop into a crippling infection. Make sure the injury is cleaned, disinfected, and wrapped at least once daily. In addition to local treatment, veterinary attention and the administration of antibiotics and anti-inflammatory drugs may be necessary to resolve infection and lessen the associated pain. Surgical removal of fractured or infected dewclaws is sometimes necessary, and is sometimes performed preventatively at very young age (three days old) for dewclaws that are abnormally large or loosely attached. Normal tight-fitting dewclaws need not be removed, as they have their purposes.

Fractures—Broken leg

Besides the risk of infection from a compound fracture, as discussed below, fractures can result in other health problems. When bones are broken in two, clots occasionally dislodge, or fatty marrow enters the bloodstream, causing circulation disorders involving the brain, lungs, heart, and other vital organs. It is thus important that you get your dog to a veterinarian if you think he has broken a bone.

Causes: Trauma.

Signs: Dog refuses to bear weight on the leg, or carries the limb. The leg may obviously be dangling, floppy, or displaced. If the skin is broken, or blood is present near the fracture site, the fracture is considered compound, and very serious because of potential bone infection which can be life-threatening. Before you panic, make sure a broken toenail is not causing the lameness, rather than a fracture. A dog will not bear weight on the affected leg if a bone is broken.

Prevention: Care, obedience, restraint, and vigilance.

Treatment: Leash and calm your dog. Fractures are painful, especially with movement. A muzzle may be needed for your safety. To determine the location and extent of a fracture, compare the affected limb with the opposite, unaffected limb. Cracked or chipped bones do not pose the serious threat that bones broken in two do. Clean and flush any wounds with sterile disinfectant solution. Use care to avoid forcing debris or hair deeper into the wound. Stabilize the dog, then stabilize the leg. Monitor and treat your dog for shock and internal injuries that can accompany fractures.

Only lower leg fractures (those below the stomach line in a standing dog) can be effectively splinted in the field. Fractures of upper leg bones (bones above dog's stomach

Although this is generally the best manner in which to carry your dog if he is hurt, you may need to make adjustments depending on the particular injury.

INJURIES

line, the humerus in the front leg, the femur in the hind) should not be splinted. If the dog can efficiently carry the injured leg, wrapping and splinting may not be needed. Wrap and splint lower leg bones that are obviously displaced.

Seek immediate veterinary care for all suspected fractures. Make sure other limbs, as well as the spine and pelvis, are uninjured before letting your dog carry a broken or injured limb.

Your dog may need to be carried. A dog is generally best held chest to chest, with one of your arms snugly under and around his neck and shoulders, and the other behind his upper hind legs, tucking them under the pelvis. Different transport strategies, depending on the severity and location of the fracture or fractures, may need to be employed if this method causes undo pain or fails to effectively stabilize the broken leg.

Special Considerations for Compound Fractures

If the skin is broken in the area of the fracture, with or without exposed bone, veterinary care should be sought as soon as possible. Absolute sterile technique is necessary in the flushing, dressing, wrapping, and splinting of compound breaks. Wash your hands and use latex gloves. When bones are broken, it is possible that arteries, veins, and nerves may be severed by splintered shards of bone, especially if the dog continues to move about, or worse, thrashes in pain or resentment at being restrained. Loss of circulation to the limb below the fracture is always a danger. If antibiotics have been dispensed by your veterinarian, they may be given as directed if you determine a compound fracture is present.

Splinting

Splints are generally used to stabilize fractures of the lower legs. Effective splinting immobilizes the joint above and below the fracture. If the joint above the break cannot be at least partially immobilized, splinting may be counterproductive. The objectives of a splint are to stabilize the fracture and align the bones. Splints that add weight below the fracture and do not stabilize the joint above the fracture have a pendulum effect and do more harm than good.

Splint Materials

One of the lightest and most easily applied splint materials is a roll of foam-padded sheet aluminum (C-Splint). Cut the material to size with scissors and then mold it to fit the contour of the injured leg. After properly fitting the splint material, pad the leg with synthetic cast padding and secure the splint with wrap. (Vetrap is easy to use and holds well. Take care that you do not apply it too tightly.)

You may have to try several times before you are able to correctly splint the leg. You may need to abandon your attempts altogether if the dog is uncooperative or because of the nature and location of the break. Be careful not to further injure the leg. DogLeggs® brand vests and slings can be very helpful.

Splinting Tips

To assure that the splint does not slide off the leg, it is often best that the leg is flexed (the joints bent), if the type of fracture allows. This bending permits the leg to be held off the ground as the dog walks. Additionally, before applying the splint, you should apply sticky tape to the hair along the length of the front and back of the leg, extended it ten inches beyond the toes. When you apply the splint over the tape, you can fold those extra ten inches back up over the splint, sticking it on securely. This will prevent the splint from sliding off the leg. For fractures that do not allow the leg to be flexed when splinted, this method is essential for holding the splint in its proper position.

Wrap synthetic cast padding, or other suitable material such as cotton, around the length of the broken leg to provide cushioning for the splint. Padding the leg before the application of the splint protects the limb and helps avoid pressure sores. It is usually best to apply too much padding, rather than too little. If the foot is incorporated within the splint, place small pieces of cotton between the toes to prevent sores and loss of circulation.

INJURIES

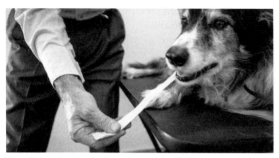

To splint a leg: 1. Apply sticky tape to the front and the back of the leg, extending it ten inches below the foot.

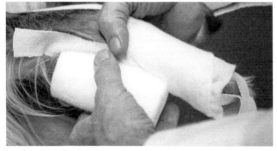

2. Wrap synthetic cast padding around the leg to provide a cushion for the splint.

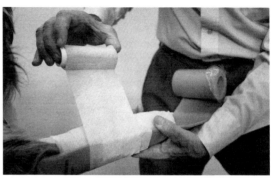

3. Apply the pre-molded splint material to the leg and fold the sticky tape up and over the cushioning, attaching it securely, to keep the splint from slipping.

Joint Troubles

Arthritis

Arthritis is inflammation of a joint, or joints. The inflammation can be from a variety of causes, age and time being the foremost. Arthritis can be acute, a sudden onset, say, or it can be chronic, long-standing. Osteoarthritis is often manageable but seldom curable, and can involve articular degeneration. Degenerative arthritis can be the result of improper growth, inadequate nutrition, previous injuries, aging, or inherited joint weakness, such as hip dysplasia (chronic arthritis of the hip joints present in many older, overweight, linebred dogs). The best prevention and treatment for arthritis is to nourish your dog with raw bones. Raw bones provide the ideal nutrients to grow and maintain strong bones and joints.

Acute arthritis has a sudden onset. It is caused by unaccustomed overactivity which overburdens one or many joints, and is especially common in dogs who are not properly acclimated to the amount of activity they will be expected to endure. Other causes of acute arthritis are trauma, such as a sprain caused by a misstep or a blow to the joint. This type of arthritis is not necessarily incurable, and minor joint injuries often resolve with rest and physical therapy, such as the application of heat or cold, and massage. Acute injuries to the bones, joints, and cartilage of a joint can result in chronic arthritis, making the joint or joints susceptible to recurrent inflammation that is worsened by exercise and cold weather.

The most unfortunate arthritis is seen in young dogs who are malnourished and then overexerted. Growing dogs are best served to eat grain-free meaty diets, supplemented with raw bones. Bone chewing enhances the soundness of wind and limb, and helps maintain a high level of dental health.

Causes: Acute arthritis—excessive activity, injuries, trauma, missteps, falls. Chronic arthritis—overnutrition for puppies; inherited tendencies (joint weaknesses such as osteochondrosis dissecans, which generally affects the shoulders, and dysplasia, which generally affects the hips); previous unresolved injuries; obesity, aging.

Signs: Limping, stiffness, lameness aggravated by exercise, joint swelling, pain when joint is flexed and extended through its range of motion.

Caution: In young growing dogs (especially larger breeds), permanent joint problems can be caused by excessive exercise and/or improper nutrition. Use care to avoid excessive activity in growing dogs. They should not be exposed to prolonged exercise to which they are not accustomed, as excessive activity can irreversibly damage growing bones and joins, as can inappropriate nutrition.

INJURIES

Stiffness and pain after workouts are usually the result of exercise's effect on a pre-existing joint problem or problems, primarily in older or obese dogs, especially those with pre-existing osteoarthritis (morning stiffness can also affect the physically unfit, but joint-normal dog). *Chronic arthritis* is often manifested as morning stiffness, worsened by unaccustomed exercise. Hip joints are prone to inflammation in large or overweight dogs; this shows up as a vague hind-end lameness or body stiffness. You can best palpate the hip joints high in the groin of a standing dog. The muscle that holds femur in its socket (the pectineus) is often inflamed, enlarged, and tender. Massage of these muscles that help hold the hip joint in place can be very helpful therapeutically and diagnostically. Locate and refer to this muscle if you have a large-breed dog.

Chronic joint conditions, while perhaps not curable, are manageable under the care and direction of a veterinarian. If your dog is experiencing stiffness after exercise, arrange for a veterinary consultation. Although I am not an advocate of x-raying every case of limping or stiffness, I am an advocate of a thorough physical exam and the institution of a physical therapy program, with consideration for appropriate, conservative use of non-steroidal, anti-inflammatory drugs (NSAIDs), which means the medicine is *not* cortisone.

Acute arthritis is the result of trauma to a formerly healthy joint, although arthritic joints can be similarly insulted, and are vulnerable to flare-ups as a result of trauma or exercise before healing is complete.

If your dog is limping for any reason, examine the leg gently and thoroughly from the toenails to the torso, checking for pain, swelling, and heat. Bend each joint through its range of motion and note your dog's response to the passive movement. If a dog resents the movement of a certain joint, it may be injured and inflamed. Compare it to other joints. Rest is always indicated for arthritis. If you are ever unsure of what to do when your dog limps, rest is the safest treatment until the dog can be examined and treated by a veterinarian.

Prevention: High-quality nutrition, appropriate conditioning, regular massage, weight control, and care with exercise, especially in young growing dogs and older aging individuals.

Treatment: Rest your dog, apply ice to acute injuries, use heat for chronic ones. Massage your dog to get in touch with the severity and location of the arthritis. If ice does not reduce inflammation, hot packing with a towel soaked in warm water with Epsom salts may be more appropriate. Anti-inflammatory drugs should be administered as directed by your veterinarian. They can play a very effective and important role in allowing your dog to exercise freely and comfortably. Medication *before* exercise is preferred in dogs with chronic arthritis. Take your older dog to his doctor to formulate an arthritis management plan before heading into the wilderness. It will make for a much more enjoyable experience for the both of you. Take your growing dog to the veterinarian to discuss nutrition and exercise regimens to encourage the critical formation of healthy joints. Aspirin is my drug of choice for my aging canine patients who get stiff following exercise. A small dose before exercise can help immensely.

Massage is great therapy to relax and relieve the muscles around the joint, as well as the muscles and joints of the unaffected legs that are subject to increased burdens. Massage is also a form of examination: It allows you to get in touch with your dog physically and emotionally and to understand where joint and muscle weaknesses are located. It also helps to develop your dog's trust in you and allows facilitation of thorough, regular musculo-skeletal examinations.

Do not indiscriminately medicate your dog with over-the-counter medications. Ibuprofen and acetaminophen are forbidden as they can cause liver and kidney damage.

Aspirin is acceptable when uncomfortable joint and muscle conditions affect your dog—5 mg per pound body weight, with food, once daily. Side effects of aspirin and other prescription NSAID arthritis medications such as Rimadyl, Duramax, Metacam, and EtoGesic are gastrointestinal upsets (vomiting and diarrhea). The use of these helpful but potent drugs should be upon the prescription and advice of your veterinarian. These drugs are toxic to the gut, kidneys, and liver and should be used conservatively and not daily. If these drugs are administered daily to manage severe pain, internal trouble will arise sooner or later. These drugs should not be given in combination. The use of aspirin precludes the concomitant use of any of the other prescription medications.

Some dogs respond well to cortisone injections, especially dogs seeking a high quality of life on their last legs of life. While there are many effective medical solutions to manage arthritis, choosing to give no medication is a fine alternative for many dogs. Medication should not be given on a constant basis, and is best tailored to the patient's individual needs upon the recommendation of your veterinarian.

INJURIES

Dislocations

A hip luxation (dislocation) is a tearing of the head of the femur out of the socket, often from a blow or fall. The round ligament and joint capsule are torn, and muscles are damaged. The hip most commonly will dislocate in an upward direction. Some dogs may have a dislocation of the hip in which ball of the hip ends up under the pelvis in the obturator foramen resulting in the dog doing the splits.

Causes: Twisting trauma to a joint, often from a blow, kick, or fall.

Signs: Limbs abnormally bent at the joint and carried in a crooked fashion; pain may or may not be present. Hip dislocations cause the dog to carry the affected leg in a floppy manner. Shoulder dislocations may present as a dragging front leg and are sometimes accompanied by nerve damage. Elbow dislocations are painful and the limb is often carried in a forward fashion. Spinal dislocations or subluxations may present with neurological signs or paralysis. The hip, shoulder, and elbow are the most frequently dislocated joints, but any joints, including the spinal, jaw, and neck joints, can be dislocated. Most all will require eventual veterinary attention, except the unusual case that somehow "pops" back in, from movement or with a proper reduction effort with educated hands.

Dislocations are easily confused with fractures and may in fact be associated with a fracture. Bent painful limbs are in the realm of veterinary medicine. Get your dog to a doctor with a reasonable urgency. The sooner a dislocated joint is returned to its socket the less likely the dislocation is to recur. General anesthesia is often required to achieve the necessary muscle relaxation to reduce (replace the joint in its socket) the dislocation.

Preventions: Proper conditioning, restraint and control of your dog in dangerous situations. Take care to avoid unstable travel on steep slopes, rocky riverbeds, and heavily timbered terrain. Keep the dog from falling out the vehicle, please. Many fractured femurs occur when dogs fall out of the back of moving pickup trucks.

Treatment: Some dislocations pop back in, or are easily reduced if one knows the anatomical angles required for reduction, the sooner the better in many instances, remembering to first do no harm. If the ball can be returned to the socket, a caudal stretching with outward rotation for craniodorsal coxofemoral luxations, the limb can be maintained in a flexed position with abduction and internal rotation sling, an Ehmer splint. When dislocated hips are reduced, they are best served to be non-weight bearing to allow the damaged internal ligaments to heal.

Again, it is nice to have a dog who willingly allows you to reduce a dislocation, although some are unlikely to tolerate the pain, thus the need for veterinary anesthesia. If you develop a close relationship with your veterinarian, it is possible for her to prescribe you an advanced first aid kit which provides appropriate pain medications and sedatives that facilitate first aid procedures. The doctor has to develop an extensive Patient/client/doctor relationship with you and your dog.

More serious or long-standing dislocations often require veterinary anesthesia and manipulation. X-rays are always welcome. Back, neck, jaw, tail, and joint dislocations cannot be easily differentiated from fractures; many require careful transport to veterinary care. With leg joint dislocations, as with some fractures, the dog may be able to carry his leg through smooth terrain. Slings may help protect the limb. When nerve damage is present, rendering the limb limp and dragging, you may want to secure the affected limb to the torso with wraps to help the dog travel if the situation so warrants. Upper joint dislocations are not amenable to splinting, but slings may help. DogLeggs® brand vests and slings can be very helpful in the first aid management of dislocations and fractures, allowing the injured leg to be carried while the dog quite ably ambulates on the other three legs. Dogs have evolved travel effectively on three limbs, as all have seen.

As for popping a joint back into place in the field, a practiced hand and a thorough knowledge of canine anatomy and physiology are prerequisite. One can always study the unaffected limb, and perhaps get an idea of the displacement and the pressures needed to get the bones back in place. Understand that fractures may complicate some dislocations.

First, do no harm.
Primum non nocere.

Damage nothing.
Nil nocere.

Dog First Aid Tip

Although not life-threatening, I consider dislocations to be emergencies. There is an urgency to reducing dislocations—the sooner they are resolved, the better. They are more easily put back in place (reduced) and are less likely to recur if treated earlier rather than later. Some require surgery for resolution.

INJURIES

Chapter 17 — Wild Animal Problems

Bites

Causes: Wildlife encounters.

Signs: Bite marks, stinky, punctures wounds, lacerations, witnessing or hearing an animal fight, quills.

Prevention: A thorough knowledge of and respect for local wildlife, as well as having a dog that willingly comes when called. Domestic dogs are best taught not to look at wildlife, to ignore wildlife, please.

Treatment: Flush bite wounds repeatedly with sterile solution or diluted disinfectant (Nolvasan, one ounce to one quart of clean water). Make sure the solution flows back out of the wound and not into a body cavity before continuing flushing. Profuse flushing is recommended, provided the flushing appears to be flushing debris and bacteria out of the wound, rather than deeper, or into a body cavity, please.

After flushing, soak puncture and bite injuries with Epsom salts in clean warm water (one handful Epsom salts per quart of warm water). If you are unable to submerge the wound site, soak the solution into a towel and hold it on the affected area for a half hour every two hours.

Do not stitch or seal punctures, as this may trap infection in deep tissues. In older wounds, encourage drainage of any pus. If wraps are not needed to control bleeding or to prevent further contamination, leave puncture wounds unwrapped to allow drainage. Flush with disinfected water several times a day. Apply hot packs as directed above. Antibiotics can be applied at the direction and discretion of your veterinarian, or given orally to manage bite wound infections, which can be nasty.

Quilled Dogs

Restrain your dog and remove the quills. Grasp the quills firmly with pliers, and pull straight away, quickly. Do not cut the quills. Take your time, as the process

Caution: Rabies transmission occurs when a rabid animal's infective saliva contacts the dog's nerves. The incubation period for rabies can be several months as the virus follows nerves to the dog's brain. The importance of rabies vaccination for all dogs cannot be overemphasized. Regular boosters are necessary to maintain immunity to this deadly disease that affects almost all mammals and man.

can be quite painful for the dog, thus sedatives may help. Double check everywhere for overlooked quills. Use feel to find the quills. Check the throat and tongue. Apparently, certain dogs try to mate with porcupines and are extensively impaled with quills everywhere. We can always tell which porcupine quilled certain dogs; the naked one. Many dogs resort to biting their guardians if the quills are attempted to be removed in a painful fashion. These dogs are the ones that show up at the veterinary clinic ready to bite anyone who moves their way.

All canids, both wild and domestic, with teeth can and will bite, as is their nature. Biting is a response to fear and pain. Some dogs will defer and allow quills to be easily removed, appreciating the value of having the quills removed, taking the pain like a hero. Other dogs cannot bear the quill-removal misery, and resort to biting people until the pain is numbed with medication.

Skunked Dogs

Causes: Encounter with spraying skunk.
Signs: Typical smell, watery eyes.
Prevention: Rabies vaccination prevents your dog from acquiring rabies during these encounters.
Treatment: Flush eyes with eye wash. Bathe daily with

Dr. Sid's special bathing remedy:
One pint hydrogen peroxide three percent
(may cause some bleaching of the hair)
One quart water
One-fourth cup baking soda
One tablespoon Prell concentrate shampoo
This mixture is said to neutralize the thiols, but skunked dogs take time to stop stinking.

Mix thoroughly and bathe once daily for seven days, adding warm water during the bath to assist sudsing. Rinse with baking soda rinse—one cup baking soda in one gallon water. Wait one-half hour and rinse again with copious amounts of warm water.

Skunk spray is composed of several low molecular weight thiols, which are responsible for the odor. These are neutralized by the hydrogen peroxide and absorbed by the baking soda. Good luck with this.

Avoid getting soap into your dog's eyes, and rinse his eyes afterwards with eyewash. Wear a rubber suit if you have one. The traditional remedies of tomato juice and vanilla are not often helpful. Repeat the bathing daily until smell is gone. Bathing with this remedy, swimming afterwards, and tincture of time will eventually resolve the smell. Nothing completely removes heavy sprayings initially.

INJURIES

61

Be sure to consider rabies, and make sure your dog was protected. Skunks are the primary purveyors of rabies in many geographic regions. Horses get rabies from being bit in the nose by a disoriented rabid skunk, fox, or raccoon. Cats get rabies from playing with a grounded rabid bat. Dogs get rabies from rabid fox encounters.

18   **Limp Tail Syndrome**

I mention this because I see it so often—occasionally outdoor dogs will develop a droopy tail from outdoor activities, especially after swimming, and the unremitting shaking that occurs to rid the hair of water each time the dog emerges from the water.

Causes: Repeated and excessive body shaking after swimming. The dog shakes so hard in his attempts to fling water from his fur that repeated stress is put on the muscles and bones at the base of the tail. Tail trauma can also cause a droopy, painful tail. Fractures, tail vertebrae dislocations, anal gland impactions, and infected bite wounds are possibilities.

Signs: Pain at the base of the tail. Diminished or painful tail wagging. Droopy, painful tail. Reluctance to sit.

Prevention: Control the amount of violent shaking by controlling the number of times the dog goes in and out of the water. Stop swimming if shaking becomes repetitively unmanageable.

Treatment: Rest your dog. Stop him from swimming. Cold or hot packs may offer relief. You can massage the base of the tail to help restore tone and tail function if your dog allows it. In cases of trauma or animal bites, veterinary attention may be appropriate. Anti-inflammatory medication is often helpful.

19 Abdominal Problems

Bloated Abdomen = Big Trouble

Causes: Twisted stomach (gastric torsion, gastric volvulus), twisted gut, abdominal infection (peritonitis), deep puncture wounds to abdomen which subsequently become infected by gas-producing bacteria.

Twisting of the stomach is most common in deep-chested breeds that exercise after eating. Food in the stomach creates a pendulum effect that combines with the side-to-side momentum brought about by exercise, and the stomach is flipped, occluding (obstructing) vessels and gut. The twist causes life-threatening circulation impairment, buildup of gas, and pressure in the abdomen which ultimately compresses the lungs and impairs breathing. The gut or stomach loses its oxygen supply. The abdomen swells, rising like bread dough. A very fast course of system failure follows, resulting in a very sick dog.

Signs: Abdominal enlargement, fullness, tight and painful stomach, snapping the finger on the abdomen makes a drumlike sound. Serious shock develops quickly, breathing becomes difficult because of the internal pressure in the diaphragm. The gums turn blue. Unproductive attempts to vomit, painful look, anxiety, dog continually gets up and down, groaning, drooling.

Abdominal enlargement can also be a result of overeating. Un-enriched dogs will sometimes eat a whole bag of dog food, given the opportunity. This is often not as serious as bloat, but the dog will look quite bloated, bloated and happy in many instances of gorging. These dogs should be getting a raw bone a day to enrich and sate their need for fresh, meaty nourishment, which often results in a more nutritionally content dog that is less likely to gorge or overeat. Unfulfilled dogs often try to eat the human food, and do.

Prevention: Avoid bloat by feeding smaller, meatier meals. Allow adequate time for the food to digest and pass from the stomach before exercising the dog. Evening feedings before the one hour evening walk are preferred to allow proper digestion through a good night's rest. Kibble in a bag is processed and difficult to digest. More digestible nutrients are frozen meat, raw bones, and freeze dried salmon. Dogs properly fed a raw, or mostly raw, diet seldom bloat.

Treatment: Pass a tube down the esophagus to relieve the gas and make arrangement to transport to veterinary hospital ASAP. This is often beyond first aid if the bloat cannot be relieved. Sometimes a trocar will relieve the distention, but the chance a big needle poked into the abdomen can cause harm, so be careful, and know where you are poking, and what, doctor.

In serious cases with rapidly deteriorating vital signs, you should attempt to pass a stomach tube through the dog's mouth to his stomach while on the way to the vet's. When the tube reaches the back of the mouth, blow softly through it to stimulate swallowing of the tube. Make sure the tube is in the stomach and not the lungs. Stomach contents and stomach gas will come out of the tube when it reaches the stomach, which may prove difficult to reach because of the twist. If the tube enters the windpipe, coughing and gagging often ensue.

In near-death cases, you can insert a needle through the abdomen into the stomach to relieve the accumulated gas and life-threatening internal pressure. You should attempt this possibly harmful procedure only on severely bloated, dying dogs.

Abdominal Pain, Belly-Ache, Gaunt or Swollen Abdomen

Causes: Various abdominal and gastrointestinal infections and insults. Unwise eating of inappropriate leftovers, dead carrion, and assorted poisons.

Ingestion of foreign bodies with the potential to puncture or saw through the gut, such as fish hooks and fishing line, pork chop bones, and certain sticks and rocks.

Signs: Frequent vomiting, listlessness, tense, tender abdomen, diarrhea, constipation, reluctance to exercise, perforating wounds of the abdomen.

Prevention: Prevent ingestion of inappropriate foods and dangerous objects.

Treatment: These issues generally require veterinary attention. Do not allow your dog to eat or excessively drink. Some dogs drink until they vomit. Prevent that, but encourage moderate drinking by allowing fifteen laps of water every five minutes, unless that brings about vomiting as well. Abdominal massage and rest may be helpful. Monitor the dog's vital signs. If they deteriorate, the condition may be serious. Seek veterinary help. Avoid indiscriminate administration of oral medication.

Abdominal Injuries

Causes: Puncture of the abdomen by sticks when running, and by bullets. Blunt trauma from falls, kicks, or vehicles.

Signs: Carefully examine the abdomen for injuries, hair loss, blood, symmetry, fluid accumulation (from internal bleeding or ruptured bladder), bulges, hernias. Some injuries are hidden in the groin area. Look carefully, as the underside of the dog is a sometimes overlooked, often hidden area. Explore the dog's torso in its entirety. Check vital signs.

Prevention: Keen vigilance of your dog's surroundings.

Treatment: Contain gaping or gut-spilling abdominal wounds initially with direct pressure after sliding skin over the opening. You may need to apply belly wraps to keep the abdominal contents in the abdomen. Use clean or gloved hands and sterile wound dressings. Avoid dumping medications into the abdomen. Flush eviscerated guts with disinfectant solution before returning them to the abdomen. If unable to return the guts, wrap in a wet towel.

All entry wounds should be cleaned, the loose hair picked away, and superficially flushed or wiped using sterile water and disinfectant. Bullet holes are often singular, small entry wounds. Exit wounds, if present, are often larger.

Seek immediate veterinary assistance for all wounds that puncture the chest or abdomen. These injuries are life-threatening.

Internal Bleeding

You may be uncertain about whether internal bleeding is present. If the gums remain pink, and the heartbeat normal, it is in all likelihood not an immediate life-threatening issue. Monitor and record the vital signs of temperature, pulse, and respiration, as well as the capillary refill times. Recheck every fifteen minutes to determine the course and extent of internal injuries. If the vital signs are deteriorating, seek immediate veterinary assistance.

Causes: Blunt trauma to the torso. Cumulative ingestion of hemorrhage-inducing rat and mouse poisons, orrats and mice killed by the poisons. (The poisons stop the blood from clotting. Vitamin K is an antidote.)

Signs: Weakness progressing to an overall limpness. Fast, weak heartbeat that increases over time. Noisy breathing, a light weak cough. Pale or muddy gums; slow capillary refill time. The onset of shock in the absence of obvious external injuries indicates internal complications requiring veterinary attendance. Shock from hemorrhage can be evaluated by measuring the vital signs, pulse over 120, rapid breathing, low temperature.

Prevention: Avoid dangerous scenarios. Use care to prevent your dog from ingesting mouse and rat poison and also the mice and rats so poisoned.

Treatment: Monitor pulse, respiration, gum color and refill, and temperature. Note improvement or deterioration. Keep your pet warm. Offer liquids. Transport the dog to a veterinarian. Administer Vitamin K.

20 Gastrointestinal Upsets

Vomiting

Causes: Change in diet, motion sickness and anxiety, kidney and liver failure, poisoning, parasitism, protozoa, extended kenneling, and bacterial intestinal infections cause the majority of diarrheas, a rather common affliction of traveling dogs.

The most common cause of vomiting and diarrhea is a change in diet—intentional or unintentional, known or unknown. Outdoor dogs have an instinctual attraction to all sorts of meaty, stinky, rotten and unfamiliar fare. A different brand of dog food (whether their own or their canine buddy's), camp foods, medications (especially anti-inflammatory drugs, see the section on joint trouble in Chapter 16), animal feces (including human), dead animals, cooked bones, sticks, pine cones, mushrooms, and rocks—you name it; unfulfilled dogs will eat it. Any unfamiliar fare can upset the gastrointestinal tract. Some dogs can handle eating indiscretions, others not so much. The digestive system rejects the insult, and the dog either throws it up or passes the unusual ingesta on through, sometimes quite dramatically. Projectile diarrhea is never a good thing. Dehydration quickly ensues. The pancreas—the organ that secretes digestive enzymes as well as insulin—can overreact to diet changes and stress and become inflamed. This results in pancreatitis, which causes excessive secretion of digestive enzymes, irritating the stomach and upper intestine and inciting unremitting stomach upset and subsequent fever and infection in some cases. Excessive salivation (drooling) is often present before and after vomiting.

Your dog's vulnerability to intestinal upset can change with time. When your dog exhibits vomiting and diarrhea, explore what he might have ingested, and investigate possible sources, eliminating them when feasible.

Signs: Drooling, vomiting, diarrhea, dehydration, inappetence, weakness. Subsequent fever and malaise.

Prevention: Keep your dog from eating what he ought not eat. This is best achieved by making sure your dog is enriched on a daily basis with safe raw meat and appropriate raw bones. When these ideal nutrients are fed on a regular basis, dogs avoid eating things they should not, knowing the best meat will be provided to them by you. Many dogs are not impressed with heavily processed kibble poured from a bag for human convenience. Their unwelcome search for things to eat is a message is that you have failed to satisfy their need for fresh meats on a regular basis. If your dog is eating things she should not, then it is time to make sure you are feeding your dog properly. Processed food, however high end, is never enough to satisfy the nutrition need in many dogs.

Treatment: If vomiting is occasional, food should be withheld for six hours to allow the intestinal tract a rest. Drinking should be allowed, provided it does not cause further vomiting, and does not become excessive or compulsive. If the dog has a tendency to overdrink, allow ten to fifteen laps every five minutes.

Continuous or unrelenting vomiting suggest serious potential consequences. Take the time to check and record the temperature, pulse, and respiratory rates hourly. Chart the direction of things. Check the gums often. If the vital signs deteriorate, consider more serious issues, including kidney and liver failure, poisoning, parasitism, ulcers, and abdominal infection, all requiring veterinary care. Head to the veterinarian, please.

Diarrhea

Causes: Change in exercise activity, routine, and diet are the most frequent causes of diarrhea *and* vomiting. Anxiety is another common cause of diarrhea. Locked in the kennel too long seems to cause diarrhea most every time it happens. The problem can range from mild to severe. In mild cases, the dog's behavior remains normal, and diarrhea subsides with rest, alleviation of anxiety, adequate hydration, and fasting.

Signs: Loose stool initially, followed by a watery, voluminous, smelly and sometimes bloody stool. Frequent bowel movements, or frequent attempts at bowel movements. Licking the rear, dragging the rear.

Prevention: Maintain dog's regular diet and avoid dietary changes. Properly enrich your dog with meat and bone before heading into the wilderness, where your dog will find his own if you have not. Avoid requiring dogs to hold their stool or urine for unusually long times. Dogs generally will not void in small kennels unless it is beyond their control. Offer your dog frequent opportunities to void. Be aware that certain infectious and toxic diarrheas can have a very fast and fatal course, especially when accompanied by intestinal or gastric torsions.

Treatment: Withhold food for a period of time. You may use oral fluids such as clear Gatorade, broth, or electrolyte/glucose replacement mixtures to help prevent the depletion of needed nutrients. Rest your dog. Reassure and calm him if he is worried or anxious. Administer DiaGel®, or a similar holistic absorbent diarrhea remedy that coats and soothes the gut while slowing it down.

After a decent fast, institute a slow and careful restoration of your dog's usual diet, and a gradual return to activity.

Bloody diarrhea associated with fever and depression indicates infectious diarrhea and the need for immediate professional care and treatment. Monitor the temperature, pulse, and respiratory rates. Record and compare them over the hours. If they continue to deteriorate, other causes such as organ failure and poisoning will require immediate veterinary treatment.

Loss of Appetite

Adequate nutrition is essential for a hiking dog. Take seriously any loss of appetite if your dog is expected to continue a strenuous routine. A day without food usually presents minimal problems, but refusal to eat for longer than thirty-six hours can result in weakness and eventual metabolic dysfunction if the dog continues to exercise. Remember to avoid high levels of activity too soon after eating. Allow time for food to digest before exercise.

Causes: Changes in accustomed exercise and dietary routine. Presence of strange people or dogs. Anxiety or physical discomforts such as bone and joint pain or abdominal upset. Ingestion of untoward substances. Burnt tongue from eating campfire food that is too hot.

Signs: Refusal to eat for longer than thirty-six hours can indicate serious illness, although some dogs can go a few days without much trouble. Always offer meat.

Treatment: Offer privacy and security when feeding your dog. Avoid intimidation by other dogs or people, intentional or otherwise. Adequate rest and reassurance may be necessary to restore his appetite. Add meat and raw bone to the diet.

You can heat dog food to make it aromatic and thus more appealing to him. The addition of warm water or bland but enticing broths may also encourage ingestion. Sometimes a dog knows when to rest his digestive tract and a lack of appetite in the face of change is not necessarily abnormal. A high level of activity, as well as apprehension and stress, shuts down the digestive system. In the absence of underlying medical conditions, when the dog's routine is normalized and fears alleviated, he should resume eating.

On the other hand, failure to eat can be associated with the onset of serious illness, especially in dogs who have never exhibited anorexia in their life (Labradors come to mind). Monitor and record your dog's vital signs during his periods of not eating. Lack of appetite can be an early sign of illness or discomfort, especially if associated with depression or listlessness. If your dog's personality changes or his constitution deteriorates, cease activity, and check his gums, temperature, pulse, and respiration. You know how to measure your dog's vital signs. This takes all the guesswork out of appreciating if the condition is getting better or worse. Seek professional help in the face of abnormal or deteriorating vital signs.

Constipation

Causes: Change in diet, ingestion of inappropriate materials and foodstuffs. Dehydration. Previous pelvic fractures and injuries that narrow the pelvic cavity. Enlarged prostate. Impacted anal glands.

Signs: Licking his rear end. Repeated unsuccessful attempts to pass a stool. This is sometimes confused with frequent attempts to urinate or difficulty in doing so.

Prevention: Avoid diet changes, make sure your dog drinks plenty during exercise and at high altitudes. Regular veterinary examinations, especially for older, unneutered male dogs (prostate issues), or those with a history of pelvic injury requiring special dietary management. Have your dog's anal glands inspected by a veterinarian in cases of excessive scooting or licking of his rear (the most common cause of these unsavory behaviors, with tapeworms a distant second).

Treatment: Encourage your dog to drink fluids (water, broth, or diluted milk).

You may want to administer a warm water enema. Using a syringe, gently push one cubic centimeter of water per pound of body weight into the rectum every four hours as needed. Fleet or other commercial enemas are preferred. Glycerin or mineral oil can be administered rectally; however, oily substances should not be forced orally as they can find their way into the lungs, causing a serious pneumonia.

Take the dog's temperature. Insertion of the thermometer will allow closer inspection of the area and reveal the nature and severity of the problem. Occasionally an ingested cooked bone or foreign body becomes lodged in the rectum as it passes through the pelvic canal. These can sometimes be retrieved, but most physical blockages require veterinary intervention. If constipation is accompanied by bloating and a deteriorating physical condition, seek veterinary care.

Dog First Aid Tip

You dog's vulnerability changes with time. That he ate three rotten whitefish this year happily and uneventfully may not tell you what he can handle next year, or even next week. When your dog exhibits gastrointestinal upsets, think change in diet, and investigate possible sources, eliminating them when feasible.

21 Eye Trouble

Pink Eye; Conjunctivitis; Sore Eye, Goopy Eye

Causes: Exposure to unaccustomed sun, dust, wind, and snow. Allergies to pollens, smoke, and plant irritants. Foreign bodies in the eye. Infectious disease (kennel cough, distemper, pinkeye, many others).

Signs: Redness and swelling of the sclera (the white of the eyeball) and the conjunctival membranes (the tissue under the eyelids). Squinting, scratching at the eyes, running the head along the ground or other surfaces in an attempt to get relief.

Prevention: Avoidance of eye irritation, regular checkups and appropriate Bordetella immunizations where indicated. Avoid conditions that threaten to injure the eyes. Ease up on letting the dog hang his head out the window, please. Quit running him through those dusty, weedy areas. Eye protection gear.

Treatment: Prevent your dog from further irritating his eyes. Avoid direct sunlight. Dogs can cause significant further injury to their eyes by rubbing their eyes along the ground or scratching at their eyes with their paws. Avoid this by leashing your dog and discouraging this behavior. Bright sun reflected off of snow can cause snow blindness and eye inflammation. Avoid extended periods of unaccustomed bright sun, especially when snow is on the ground.

Flush the eye with an eye-irrigating rinse, an isotonic, buffered solution formulated specifically for flushing eyes, such as sterile eye wash. Human products are often acceptable. Flushing and rinsing the eye most often requires restraint. Direct a gentle stream under the upper and lower eyelids, as well as under the third eyelid in the inside corner of the eye. You also may carefully apply

When eye issues are present, carefully examine under the eyelids, and, by pressing under the eye, examine the third eyelid for the presence of foreign bodies such as grass seeds and dirt.

eye ointments dispensed by your veterinarian. If the cornea has been damaged, do not apply an eye ointment containing cortisone (an ingredient that often ends with the suffix-one), as its use can delay or impair healing.

You can fashion a see-through head wrap out of wrapping gauze to protect the affected eye from sun and wind. Avoid exposing the dog to dust, irritants, wind, snow, and especially bright sunlight. Remove allergens and irritants from the environment and haircoat. Sometimes weeds and burrs that stick in the hair scratch the eyes.

Eye Trauma

Causes: Corneal abrasions and ulcers, foreign bodies in the eye, chemical or plant irritants, skunk spray. Self-mutilation by the dog in an attempt to relieve eye pain.

Signs: Squinting, rubbing, pawing, and fretting about the eye, causing more irritation in doing so. Foreign bodies under the eyelids and under the third eyelid.

Corneal cloudiness follows corneal abrasions, but the opacity usually takes at least a day to develop. A normal cornea is clear and smooth as glass.

Prevention: Avoid travel in eye-stabbing scenarios. Prevent your dog from digging at his eyes. Avoid aggressive felines.

Treatment: Corneal injuries and acquired defects benefit greatly from prompt veterinary care, lessening the likelihood of permanent corneal scarring.

Remove loose foreign bodies by restraining the dog and washing out the foreign body with eyewash. Use a wet cotton swab to lure out debris that will not flush. *Do not use tweezers or forceps or other instruments that could impale or further damage the eye if the dog flinches.*

Avoid further irritation (tall grass or weeds, wind, dust) and keep your dog shaded from direct sunlight. Use care and good judgment before patching or wrapping an eye. Reserve wrapping for severely injured eyes and those requiring direct pressure to control bleeding or expulsion of the eye or eye contents. If wrapping is necessary, flush lightly, place sterile gauze over the eye, and place the wrap loosely over head and under the jaw. Seek medical attention.

Watery, Weepy Eyes

Causes: Allergies, infections, or mild trauma. Dental disease. Poor eyelid conformation, such as droopy eyes (ectropion) that collect dust and debris or turned-in eyelids (entropion) where the eyelashes rub and irritate the cornea. Excessive tearing or gooping of the eyes can signal the onset of viral diseases, allergies, pinkeye bacterial infection, and other irritating eye conditions.

Signs: Wetness about the eyes, frequent blinking, squinting, and pawing at the eyes.

Prevention: Avoid eye irritants such as dust, pollinating plants, and wind. Regular checkups and eye examinations.

Treatment: Flush the eye with eyewash. In the case of poor eyelid conformation, surgery may be necessary.

Cherry Eye

The immune tonsil-like lymphoid tissue underneath the third eyelid becomes inflamed. This condition is common in spaniels, but it is not limited to those breeds.

Causes: Chronic irritation or infection. Dental disease of the teeth below the eye.

Signs: Third eyelid noticeably inflamed, exhibiting a cherry-like appearance on the inside of the eye next to the nose.

Prevention: Avoid activities, allergens, smokes, and dry plants that threaten to irritate reactive eyes. Premedicate the eyes as directed by your veterinarian before venturing outdoors. Make sure your dog's teeth are as white and clean as yours, and that dental disease is not present. Bad breath is abnormal, and often indicates dental disease.

Treatment: Flush the eye and make certain there is no foreign body under the third eyelid. Avoid further eye irritation. Cases commonly recur and require veterinary treatment. Surgical removal of the lymphoid tissue is often effective, but the validity of the procedure is debated by some veterinary ophthalmologists. Make sure dental disease is resolved if it is present.

Caution: In most cases foreign bodies that impale the eyeball should be left in place while the dog is immediately transported to a veterinarian. Wrapping, or attempting to wrap the eye ofter causes further trauma. Just get to the doctor.

22 Ear Problems

Ear Canal Problems

Causes: Ear infection (yeast, bacteria), foreign bodies in ear canal (awns, seeds), ear mites, water in the ear, lack of ventilation (excessive hair under the ear flaps and around the ear), hair growing and accumulating in the ear canal.

Narrow or restrictive ear canal anatomy. Allergies of all types, especially food allergies. Hypothyroidism and other internal medical disorders. Cheap treats, milk bones, and inappropriate foods often incite ear inflammation, so avoid these.

Signs: Head shaking and ear scratching. Dirty, smelly, red ear canals. Discharge in the ear canal that collects on the hair about the ears. The dog may tilt his head to the side of the affected ear. Awns (grass seeds) in the surrounding hair.

Prevention: Ear yeast and bacteria prefer dark, moist environments. Attempt to keep your dog's ears ventilated, cleaned, and dry. Avoid letting him swim. Clip the hair from under the ear and around the ear canal opening so the hair does not attract awns or prevent good ventilation. Frequent hair removal and ear cleaning prevent ear infections. Have recurrent or unremitting ear problems addressed by your dog's doctor.

Avoid feeding inexpensive dog food.

Treatment: Carefully remove debris with Q-tips. Use extreme care to avoid pushing hair, gunk, or foreign bodies down into the ear canal. Attempt to get around the debris before drawing it out of the ear.

Flush the ear canal with ear wash or clean water. Do not use full strength alcohol or hydrogen peroxide. Medicate with an ear ointment as prescribed by your veterinarian. If the condition worsens or is unresponsive to cleaning, veterinary attention is necessary— the sooner the better.

If the ears are excessively painful, anti-inflammatory medication dispensed by your veterinarian will reduce swelling and pain, allowing better cleaning after it has taken effect. Repeat cleanings are often necessary,

EYES, EARS, MOUTH

providing the procedure does not cause further irritation. Veterinary care is often needed to resolve ear infections and to prevent them from recurring in the future.

Serious Middle and Inner Ear Infections

More serious and deeper ear infections or injuries affect the vestibular apparatus of the middle ear causing balance disorders. A head tilt towards the affected ear can occur with a middle or inner ear infection. Loss of balance and difficulty walking may indicate serious, deep-seated ear disorders. Immediately seek a veterinarian's care if these serious signs are present.

Swollen Ear Flaps (Aural Hematomas)

Causes: Excessive head shaking due to a foreign body or infection of the ear canal. Trauma, such as dog-fight bite. Swelling results from a broken blood vessel between the skin and ear cartilage.

Signs: Bulges or swelling in the earflaps, often oblong, golf-ball size or larger, sometimes fluctuant, sometimes hard.

Prevention: Prevent ear infections and head shaking. Always examine the ear canal in cases of head shaking or unusual body odor.

Treatment: Resolve the ear irritation or infection as described above to stop the cause of the head shaking. To prevent further swelling, wrap the ear to the head to stop internal bleeding and prevent additional damage from head shaking. See your veterinarian. The condition may require drainage or surgery, but is not often serious or life-threatening, but can be quite burdensome to some dogs. The blood and serum can be drained from the ear using a 16 or 18 gauge needle, and the ear can then be secured to the head with a wrap.

The underlying ear issue that caused the head shaking to burst the vessels in the ear flap can be more serious that the hematoma. This hematoma, if persistent, may require veterinary surgery to resolve, but this is not usually an emergency situation. The first-aid objectives are to prevent further head shaking by resolving the cause of the shaking and to secure the ears to prevent further damage. The ear canal should be gently cleaned, flushed, and medicated. If there are foreign bodies such as grass seeds or awns in the ear canal, they should be removed.

23 Dental Troubles

Broken, Rotten, Loose, or Dislocated Tooth

Learn the difference between adult and baby teeth from your veterinarian. Growing dogs shed (or sometimes break off) baby teeth, a normal condition.

You should consider jaw fractures or dislocations if you find broken or misplaced teeth. Check for symmetry of the teeth, comparing the teeth on the opposite side of the mouth. Observe the dog's ability to close his mouth as well as his bite (upper and lower tooth alignment). Note any resistance, pain, or improper positioning when passively opening and closing the jaws. Check the inside of the mouth for associated injuries. Examine the tongue, above and below.

Causes: Head trauma, kicks, falls, rock retrieving, and eating or chewing hard objects. Pre-existing dental disease.

Signs: Mouth pain or bleeding, nosebleeds, refusal to eat. Unusual tongue and jaw movements. Bad, bad breath.

Prevention: Regular dental examinations and cleanings (dental disease is the most common medical disorder I see in dogs). Brushing and chewing (appropriate chewing is great for your dog's medical, physical, and dental health). Avoid situations that may result in head trauma, such as chasing horses, etc.

Treatment: Loose *adult* teeth should be repositioned to their normal placement, if possible. Do not let your dog chew or eat. Offer a liquid diet until veterinary attention is available.

If more than a third of the tooth is broken off, sensitive tissue is often exposed. The remaining tooth should be disinfected with hydrogen peroxide using a cotton swab. The hydrogen peroxide helps stops the bleeding, but should be used sparingly.

Associated trauma can cause holes in the cheek or palate. Sometimes the jaw joint is injured, or the jaw broken. Dogs have evolved a significant ability to maintain dental integrity despite broken teeth. Many broken teeth resolve without treatment, or are not noticed until well after the injury has occurred. If the bite is abnormal, the jaw may be dislocated, and nerves to the tongue and throat might be impaired, making eating or drinking difficult or impossible. A veterinarian should examine all dogs that have dental injuries. You can sometimes use a muzzle to stabilize a severely broken-up mouth while you seek veterinary care.

EYES, EARS, MOUTH

Mouth Sores

Signs: Drooling, refusal to eat, digging at mouth with paws, rubbing face along the ground.

Causes: Dental disease. Electrical shocks from chewing through electrical cords, burns inside the mouth from eating hot food, injuries from chewing or fetching sharp objects, animal bites, head trauma, porcupine quills.

Prevention: Avoid inappropriate chewing. Regular dental exams.

Treatment: Flush mouth with sterile saline or eye wash. Do not feed your dog, but do encourage him to drink. Swab cuts and sores with hydrogen peroxide on a Q-tip. Certain metabolic conditions (kidney failure) or drugs (in particular, anti-inflammatory drugs) can cause oral sores and erosions. Seek veterinary care.

24 Tick and Insect Trouble

Ticks

Ticks can transmit serious, sometimes incurable diseases to dogs and people and in rare cases, cause paralysis or other neurologic and infectious disease. If you find a tick on yourself, carefully check your dog, and vice versa.

Causes: A variety of ticks (eight-legged *Acarina* species).

Signs: Obvious ticks embedded and engorged in your dog's skin, often under the ears and neck. Close inspection of your dog can reveal odd swellings and bumps to be feeding ticks. Be aware of the possibility of subsequent tick-borne diseases, including but not limited to Lyme disease, Rocky Mountain Spotted Fever, tick paralysis, and others—ticks are nasty little disease vectors. See your veterinarian and medical doctor after all dug-in tick encounters.

Prevention: Tick repellents can be obtained through your veterinarian depending on where your dog travels. Follow the advice of your dog's doctor. First, identify if the problem even exists. Flea and tick products are potent, toxic chemicals. Dogs that exercise rigorously are more susceptible to their side effects, especially after recent application. Do not apply these products unless their use is clearly indicated by your veterinarian, such as in certain areas during certain times of the year, and certainly do not use them for every foray into the woods unless a serious risk is present, which may be the case in some, but not all parts, of the country.

Treatment: Ticks most frequently dig in under the neck and around the ears. Use care and cleanliness in handling ticks and other parasites. If you encounter a tick, check the entire dog, every nook and cranny, for others. Check your own body as well. With tweezers, forceps, or gloved fingers remove the tick by grasping the tick as close to the skin as possible and pulling the tick straight out. Do not apply ointments, salves or hot matches to the tick trying to get them to back out. This may cause the tick to regurgitate toxins into the skin. It is generally believed that ticks do not ingest toxins until they have been attached for 24 hours. It is important that you inspect your dog for ticks after every outing and remove them before they have attached or not long after. Trying not to rip off the head. Although it is preferred that the head be removed, it is not the end of the world if it breaks off, and seldom causes a grave medical problem, short of serious disease transmission. Have your veterinarian check tick-removal sites and give the dog a physical, and consult him regarding tick diseases and possible prophylactic treatment.

Fleas and Lice

Causes: Contact with wild animals, dead or alive, or contact with other dogs or where they've been such as prairie dog infested areas, boarding kennels or veterinary hospitals (of all places).

Signs: Some dogs develop a flea-bite allergy and itch profusely. Certain lice also cause itching, although both fleas and lice can be present without itching. Not all itching dogs have fleas. Careful examination of the haircoat and underlying skin can reveal fleas and/or lice if they are present.

Prevention: Consult your veterinarian as to the appropriateness and proper use and application of a wide variety of flea preventives and remedies. Do not poison your dog with these remedies, especially when the dog is expected to do subsequent extensive strenuous exercise. Use very light dose, or half-doses of these potent insecticides. Do not use these drugs when they are not needed. For example in Montana there are no flea or heartworm issues in my practice area. Dogs visiting Montana and Yellowstone Park get a reprieve from relentless chemical use they are exposed to in other areas of the country.

Treatment: Do not indiscriminately use flea and tick medications. Do not assume fleas and ticks are everywhere, they are not. If you are forced to use over-the-counter products, shampoos are preferred to collars or spot-on applications, which can be toxic to working dogs and collie types. Carefully read the directions and precautions. Leave flea shampoos on your dog for at least ten or fifteen minutes so they can do their work. Then rinse *thoroughly*. See your veterinarian for definitive resolution and prevention of these and other ectoparasite (parasites that live on the outside) as the dog needs to be treated. Many animals return to the source of infection and get re-infected, much to your treating veterinarian's chagrin. Life cycles of these ectoparasites need to be understood and addressed for successful control. Aromatic oils work well to prevent infestations in many, but not all, areas.

Insect Bites and Other Skin Irritants

Causes: A variety of insect and spider bites. Plant allergies. Thistles, thorns, and cockleburs. Some plant parts can poke the animal.

Signs: Skin swellings, redness, and rashes.

Prevention: Avoidance of nasty plants and biting insects. Insect repellents in the form of aromatic oils are safest for the dog and quite effective.

Treatment: Wash inflamed areas with mild soap and water. Apply cold packs and baking soda poultices. After Bite® insect bite treatment with baking soda is effective for mosquito bites and be stings. Oral antihistamines dispensed by a veterinarian for vulnerable dogs can be helpful for swelling and hot spots. Bee stings can leave a stinger, which can be removed with a pair of tweezers, perhaps after the hair is clipped. Consult with your veterinarian regarding certain risks your dog may be, or may have been, exposed to. Cortisone creams can reduce swelling when applied topically. Aspirin can be administered at the dose of 50 mg per 20 pounds twice daily with food.

25 Poisonings

Causes: Human-induced poisonings with pesticides (flea and tick collars, spot-ons treatments), antifreeze, herbicides, rat poison (Vit K inhibitors), 1080 (sodium fluroacetate), strychnine (often as poisoned oats or in poisoned rodents), and to a lesser degree chocolate, oral fat-emulsified marijuana, and illicit or prescription drugs including ibuprofen, acetaminophen, opiate painkillers, tranquilizers, and many others. Do not assume human drugs are okay for dogs. Some are, many are not. Oral marijuana poisoning has become common with the legalization of the drug. Oral preparations such as marijuana cookies and oils can cause significant toxicity in dogs. Drooling, twitching, wobbliness and other behavioral signs can occur when these products, even in relatively small quantities, are ingested by dogs.

Ingested wild mushrooms are the most common plant poisoning, although we know now mushrooms are more closely related to animals than plants, yes. Outdoor plants that can be toxic but are usually mild unless large quantities are ingested include delphinium (larkspur), skunk cabbage, raisins, foxglove, western yew, lily, chokecherries, loco, lupine pods, rhubarb leaves, belladonna, and many others. Plants that can be very toxic include water hemlock root, camas root, and castor bean. Most plant eating causes vomiting and diarrhea from irritation rather than outright poisoning.

Signs: Vomiting, staggering, unusual behavior, bloating, diarrhea, seizures, slobbering, inability to locomote normally. If any of these signs are present, prompt action is required. The sooner the poisonous substance is eliminated from the dog, the better. The natural reaction to vomit up the toxins should be encouraged. Diarrhea is another bodily response to eliminate toxins. Once the toxin becomes absorbed, fluid therapy can help flush out the poison.

Prevention: Avoid areas where poisons are likely—automobile businesses, manufacturing areas, houses under construction, areas known to have poisonous mushrooms, etc. Do not let your pet eat unknown plants where poisonous plants are known to exist. Exotic houseplants are often a factor in poisonings. Most grasses are not a problem and occasional grazing of a little bit of green grass is a normal activity of dogs, but beware of recently sprayed areas. Keep your dog enriched with fresh meats and raw bones to reduce her tendency to seek out unwelcome things to eat. A raw bone a day minimizes untoward eating of unwelcome things. Meat sates a dog's appetite, while kibble may not.

Treatment: Attempt to identify the poison. Induce vomiting with oral hydrogen peroxide, one ounce per twenty pounds body weight, to evacuate any ingested material remaining in the stomach. Call your veterinarian and/or poison control center for advice and proper first-response action if the toxin can be identified. If signs do not lessen, take your dog to the veterinary hospital. Vitamin K is the antidote for most rodent poisons. Atropine is considered the universal antidote, but should be administered upon the advice of your veterinarian. Activated charcoal can be given orally to absorb any toxins remaining in the intestine, one ounce per twenty pounds body weight, after vomiting has been induced, or unsuccessfully induce. This can be given after vomiting has been induced, or if induction of vomiting is unsuccessful. Take care to avoid getting oral medications down the trachea and into the lungs.

Caution: Oral remedies cannot be administered safely to severely depressed, spastic (experiencing seizures), or comatose dogs.

BITES & POISON

Induce vomiting if:

- The poison ingested was noncorrosive, non-volatile and recently ingested

Administer 10 cc. hydrogen peroxide orally per 30 lbs. of weight. Repeat in 15 minutes if no vomiting occurred.

or

1 tsp. ipecac per 20 lbs of body weight.

Do not induce vomiting if:

- The dog swallowed a petroleum product, antifreeze, cleaners, strong acid or alkali, or a sharp object.
- If hours have passed since the poison was ingested.

Administer Toxiban, 1 cc. per pound of body weight every half hour for three treatments.

or

Give activated charcoal to absorb the poison

or

1 tsp. Milk of Magnesia per 10 lbs. of body weight.

26 Snake Bites

Causes: Rattlesnakes, coral snakes, copperheads, cottonmouths, and others.

Signs: A sudden yip. Swelling often occurs quickly at site of poisonous snakebites, often a leg or the nose. Head bites result in drooling, leg bites cause limping. If snake can be seen or heard, this helps confirm the problem. Examine entire dog for pain or bleeding.

Prevention: Become familiar with any poisonous snakes that frequent the area you may be traveling—rattlesnakes, coral snakes, copperheads, cottonmouths, and others. Be able to identify them. Research their behavior, environmental preferences, night or day activity, and lifestyles so as to avoid encounters. There is a *Crotalaria* vaccine that reduces the effect of rattlesnake venom, it is claimed. Some people have their dog shocked with electricity in the presence of a de-fanged rattlesnake, but I prefer something less brutal than electricity is used to teach aversion to snakes, like water spraying instead of a shock.

Treatment: If the snakebite wound is fresh and can be found, treat as follows: Wash and soak the wound to flush the venom out, using thorough, copious flushing with cold water. Wash and soak it again. Clip the hair from the bite wound and attempt to milk any surface venom out, by massaging downward from above the bite. Suction may be helpful, using the suction cups in a snakebite kit, but hair often precludes their effective use. Thorough flushing with cold water dilutes the venom and slows its absorption. Placing the leg in a clean cold stream may help. Keep the dog as calm as possible and spare him any strenuous physical activity (carry him to a veterinarian).

Depending on the amount of poisonous venom injected into the dog, he may become depressed as time wears on. Dogs, because of their relatively small size, are very vulnerable to poisonous snake bites.

In suspected snake bites where the initial bite was not observed, the bite area swells and the dog becomes listless. Apply Epsom salt compresses. Add a handful of Epsom salts to a quart of warm water, saturate a towel with the mixture, and hold it to the affected area for fifteen minutes every two hours.

Seek veterinary care. Intravenous cortisone, antivenom, and fluids will be administered. (In order to give the correct antivenom, your vet will want to know details about the size and type of snake, so be as observant as you can.) Antihistamines are contraindicated. If you travel

BITES & POISON

in known snake country, see your veterinarian ahead of time. She will dispense any necessary medications and give explicit instructions for their use.

Dog First Aid Tip

Do not cut or needle the skin at the site of the bite, despite what you may have heard to the contrary, this is not proper treatment for snake bite (not to mention that is puts you at risk of being bitten yourself—by your dog.)

27 Fish Hook and Line Problems

Fish Hooks

Causes: Fishermen and fisherwomen who are careless with their casting techniques, improper storage of hooks.

Signs: Hook embedded in the skin or mouth.

Prevention: Do not leave hooks about, especially hooks baited with liver for catfish.

Treatment: Have an assistant restrain the dog with a half nelson stretch. Hook removal hurts the dog, so be sure he is properly restrained before starting.

Wash your hands and disinfect the area.

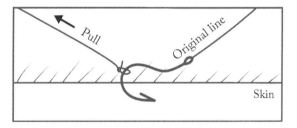

Fish hook removal—dog gently but firmly restrained.
1. Apply line to curve in hook.
2. Keep gentle tension on original line to stabilize the hook.
3. Pull applied line with a quick hard jerk to dislodge imbedded hook.

If the hook enters and exits the skin and the barbed portion is visible beyond the exit area, clip the barbed portion off with wire cutters and roll the hook out from its entry wound.

If the barbed portion is imbedded in flesh, tie or loop a strong line around the bend in the hook. Press down on the eye of the hook, and give the line one hard yank away from the entry site. Alternatively, hemostats can be used to grasp and remove the hook, but this can be a slower, more painful process.

If several attempts are unsuccessful or the dog resorts to biting you, abandon the attempt and head to the vet.

Line or Wire Encirclage

Encirclage is the wrapping of line or wire around a limb, or occasionally the neck, of a dog. Sometimes line wrapped around limbs is hidden in the hair or becomes imbedded in the flesh before anything is noticed. Limping and swelling become apparent when the line tightens. Exercise can worsen the condition and cause the line to become further imbedded.

Causes: Fishline or wire that wraps around limb or neck. Collars that shrink or become too small for growing dogs can create neck sores.

Signs: Limping. Swelling of affected limb. A bad smell

is sometimes the first sign of encirclage.

Prevention: Do not leave hooks and line unattended or baited.

Treatment: Restrain your dog and attempt to lift the wrapped line away from the body with tweezers, hemostats, scissors, or a barbless dulled fish hook. Clip or untie the line and remove it. Clipping the hair, cleaning the area, and soaking may facilitate locating and cutting the string. After the line is removed, flush and soak the area. Rest the dog. If swelling persists or the dog has no feeling below the encirclage, seek veterinary treatment.

Caution: Do not pull on a swallowed fish-hook line or cut all of the line away. If the hook and/or line are swallowed, it is very unlikely you will be able to successfully or safely remove it. Prevent your dog from eating anything, and seek veterinary care.

28 Porcupine Quills

Causes: Encounters with porcupines or their European relative, the hedgehog.

Signs: Obvious quills stuck in the skin, less obvious quills in the legs or paws (often accompanied by limping), quills in the mouth or tongue.

Prevention: Awareness in porcupine country.

Treatment: Restrain your dog. Remove individual quills by grasping with a pliers or similar grasping instrument (hemostat, needle holders, pocket tool, pliers, etc.) and giving a quick pull in the opposite direction of the impalement. Once the quill is grasped, jerk it out quickly, straight away and sharply. If the quills are in loose skin, hold the skin down as you pull the quill to prevent nearby quills from getting sucked under the skin. Loosely imbedded quills can be removed in bunches, lessening the overall pain of the removal procedure, which can be significant and cumulative, creating vicious resentment in your dog. Do not cut quills in half. This does not help in removal but, rather, makes them more difficult to grasp and remove, and facilitates their inward progress, which is undesirable.

Be forewarned that some quillings are extremely forceful, and quills deeply imbedded in the chest and elsewhere can migrate to cause subsequent serious complications.

Remove all visible quills. Thoroughly examine the inside of your dog's mouth. The sooner quills are removed, the more unlikely they are to migrate or become swallowed, infected, or broken off.

Some dogs do not allow quills to be removed, nor do they allow restraint for removal. Affected dogs can usually travel on their own. Limping indicates there may be quills in the legs. Watch for repeated swallowing, limping, and self-mutilation while transporting the dog to professional care.

Caution: Do *not* remove quills impaling the eyeball (seek emergency care).

Do not allow eating, drinking, or pawing at the quills. Check the feet, legs, and rest of the body for stray quills. Removal of large numbers of quills from uncooperative, biting dogs often requires veterinary assistance.

Carefully examine your dog in the days and weeks following a quilling to check for migrating quills or quill sections that may have been broken off, hidden, or overlooked, even if a doctor removed the quills. Some quills hide, and are not initially found and removed, despite everyone's thorough inspection. Carefully dispose of removed quills so that others are not inadvertently stuck.

Some dogs roll in dead porcupines. The dog stinks of a dead animal and the quills are loosely imbedded, if not simply stuck in the hair. Live porcupines emit a musk, similar to that of a skunk.

Caution: Your dog may not allow you to remove the quills, as it is very painful. I warn you that he may try to bite you, regardless of your firm belief that he would never bite anyone. Use serious premeditated restraint. The best restraint position is the stretching half nelson. A muzzle is recommended, using care in its application to avoid impinging on quills in the muzzle or inside the mouth.

CHAPTER

29 Exposure to Cold

Frostbite

Dogs perspire from the edges of their pads. Exertion in cold, snowy weather results in the perspiration freezing into iceballs that cling on the hairs around the pads and between the toes. In subzero conditions, this can lead to frostbite of the feet. Other areas prone to frostbite are the lower flanks and the sheath of male dogs.

Causes: Buildup of ice between the toes in subzero temperatures. Inadequate nutrition for the conditions. Exhaustion.

Signs: Frozen body parts. Dog alternately carrying one foot or another. Skin whitish and hard and frozen to the touch. Ears can become frozen, as can the prepuce, hocks, and tail.

Prevention: Clip the hair between the toes to minimize the buildup of ice. The likelihood of frostbite is lessened by acclimatizing your dog to cold conditions. You may opt to use properly fitting booties on the dog. Adequate nutrition and frequent drinking are important in avoiding frostbite and exhaustion. Keep in mind that cold, bitter weather increases fluid and nutritional demands and plan accordingly.

Treatment: If the area can be subsequently dried, soak the frozen tissue in cool, then warm (but not hot), water.

Dry the area and lightly massage it. Provide warmth, nourishment, and rest.

You can administer anti-inflammatory drugs as prescribed by your veterinarian to help restore circulation and minimize the pain and swelling of thawing. Enteric coated aspirin can be given at 2.5 mg/lb every twelve hours. Aspirin should not be given with other anti-inflammatory drugs.

Hypothermia

Causes: Exhaustion in cold or wet weather. Inadequate nutrition. Underlying illness.

Signs: Dizzy, weak, and cold dog, especially after long exertion and exposure to bitter conditions. The dog's

---

Dog First Aid Tip

Dogs really don't get mild colds like people. If a dog has a runny nose and gobs of goop in his eyes and is not feeling well, this is often a sign of serious disease, especially if accompanied by a fever. Call your veterinarian whenever you dog has signs of a "cold" accompanied by ill health.

temperature is subnormal. Hydration is measured by feeling inside the mouth, which should be wet and warm, rather than dry and cold.

Prevention: Adequate conditioning, warmth, and nutrition. Attention to and knowledge of pre-existing medical conditions (regular checkups).

Treatment: Protect your dog from the elements, supply warmth, and give him a full body massage. Provide fluids and nourishment. It is important that you allow your dog to rest before proceeding. Repeated bouts of weakness may indicate the presence of underlying metabolic conditions or altitude sickness. Warmed subcutaneous fluids such as Lactated Ringers can be given, 100cc per ten pounds, or until dog becomes hydrated.

Starvation

Dogs lost in the wilderness can become undernourished.

Causes: Lack of food during exposure to unfamiliar and adverse elements. Inability to digest or assimilate food in the presence of diarrhea, blockages, parasitism, and other GI maladies.

Signs: Weakness, gaunt look, sunken eyes, drawn up, empty abdomen, weight loss. Ataxia, disorientation, seizures.

Prevention: Vigilance during outdoor travel (keep track of your dog, train him not to chase deer or other wildlife for miles and miles—this happens!). Make sure your dog has proper identification on his collar. Feed your dog high quality nutrients with fresh meats during strenuous travel.

Treatment: Dogs weary from lack of food or exposure to the elements should be gradually warmed and gently massaged. Offer water in limited quantities so the dog does not overdrink and then vomit. Allow twenty laps every five minutes. You can add a pinch of salt and sugar to each cup of water. Low-sodium salt with potassium chloride (Lite Salt) is preferred. Follow the dog's fluid intake with small quantities of high-quality food; begin with ten pieces of kibble. High quality, grain free canned diets can along with fresh meats can aid in recovery after prolonged food deprivation.

Subcutaneous sterile isotonic fluids such as Lactated Ringers can be administered. Oral honey and sugars can provide energy. Kibble dog food should not be fed, as it is too difficult to process and assimilate. Meaty gruels and broths should be offered.

After stabilizing your dog, seek veterinary care to treat the problems arising from undernourishment and exposure. At times, the kidneys and liver and other internal organs may need veterinary attention.

EXPOSURE

CHAPTER 30 Heat Exposure

Heat Stroke

Causes: Overexertion in hot weather for obese, aged, inexperienced, metabolically diseased, or under-conditioned dogs. Healthy dogs running in hot weather are not spared this syndrome, either. Locked in hot car or truck. Dehydration, pre-existing illness.

Signs: Weakness, refusal to continue exercise, inability to move, frantic panting, bright red tongue, muscular weakness, collapse. Severe signs include paralysis, bloody diarrhea, unremitting panting, and glassy eyes.

Prevention: Allow for plenty of rest and fluids in hot going. Gradually condition and accustom your dog to arid conditions.

Treatment: Reduce your dog's temperature by bathing him in cool water and evaporating the water with cool air. Provide shade. Monitor the dog's temperature and other vital signs. If the vital signs deteriorate, it may be necessary to submerge him in cool water to reduce his core body temperature. Take care to not let any water near his head. Offer electrolyte water to restore proper muscle and nervous function. Seek veterinary assistance if your dog's condition does not improve.

Dehydration

Causes: Lack of frequent opportunity to drink. Persistent vomiting or diarrhea also leads to dehydration and electrolyte imbalance which can be life-threatening. Excessive exercise at high elevations or hot weather can also lead to rapid water loss. External or internal bleeding can cause dehydration as can toxemia, twisted guts, heat prostration, high altitude exertion, and shock. Dehydration is often secondary to other serious diseases. Seek veterinary assistance.

Signs: Weakness; dry, sticky gums. Excessive thirst may or may not be present, depending on the underlying cause or causes. When the skin over the back is pinched together, it tents when released and remains in this tented position, slowly returning to its original position rather than immediately falling back as it would in the normal hydrated dog. The eyes become sunken, often manifested by the third eyelid creeping over the eyeball, giving a hollow look and forlorn expression.

Prevention: Give your dog plenty of rest and offer water frequently.

Treatment: Rest your dog and administer liquids. If vomiting is the cause, wait for the vomiting to subside before offering water. Electrolyte and glucose formulations such as Gatorade or Pedialyte can be used to restore the loss of fluid, minerals, and carbohydrates. Immediate veterinary assistance should be sought if rehydration is unsuccessful and diarrhea and vomiting persist or are accompanied by a fever or low body temperature. Refer to the sections on diarrhea and vomiting in Chapter 20 for further treatment and first aid advice.

Burns and Smoke Inhalation

Causes: Campfires, stoves, wildfires, hot springs, hot cookware. The feet and tongue are most commonly affected.

Signs: The acrid smell of burnt hair, yelping during the incident, coughing, watery eyes, singed hair.

Prevention: Use care to prevent fires of all sorts. Wind can fan the deadest of coals to flame.

Treatment of Minor Burns: Rinse with cool water; repeat frequently. Clean gently with diluted disinfectant when contamination is apparent. Apply a cold washcloth. Protect the site from sun and the elements. If necessary, gently wrap the burn with non-adherent dressings. Do not use iodine or medicated powders that interfere with hydration of the skin. I am not in favor of using any medications you are unsure about. If in doubt, use nothing, certainly not butter or grease. Burns of the tongue from lapping or gulping hot food or grease can take weeks to heal. First aid for tongue burns is to seek veterinary care. They are serious.

Treatment of Severe Burns: Maintain the dog's hydration with oral fluids. Do not apply medication unless it is specifically labeled for severe burns. Protect the area from contamination with non-adherent dressings and light wraps. Extensive burns require veterinary attention to prevent life-threatening shock and toxemia. Transport treatment includes gentle cleansings with mild disinfectant solutions. For recent burns, apply cold washcloths or ice for 30 minutes. Gently blot out debris and apply a thin layer of Thermazine Silver Sulfadiazine 1% cream. Encourage your dog to drink plenty of fluids; add a pinch of salt and a pinch of sugar to each cup of water offered. The sooner professional care is obtained, the better.

Treatment of Smoke Inhalation: Smoke inhalation may cause swelling of the airways and severe coughing and retching. Gentle chest massage and mouth-to-nose resuscitation may be necessary if the dog has collapsed. Rest is essential to minimize heavy breathing. Seek veterinary care when the dog stabilizes. Provide oxygen if available. Inhalers and antihistamines may be helpful, as directed by your veterinarian.

EXPOSURE

Sunburn of the Nose (Collie Nose)

Causes: Overexposure to sunlight in sensitive, white nosed dogs.

Signs: Redness and swelling of unpigmented skin along the top of the nose.

Prevention: Apply sunscreen to unpigmented areas before setting out. Repeat as needed. Avoid excessive exposure to sunlight for sensitive dogs. Wind and snow-reflected sunlight aggravate the condition.

Treatment: Minimize or prevent any further direct sunlight. Apply cold water compresses. Apply Thermazine salve to affected skin in severe cases.

First Aid Contents
Adventure Medical Kits Workin' Dog

Instruction / Instrument
- 1 Pet First Aid Field Booklet
- 1 Headlamp, LED
- 1 Leash, 5' Nylon
- 1 Survive Outdoors Longer® Emergency Blanket 56" x 84"
- 1 Splinter Picker/Tick Remover Forceps
- 1 EMT Shears 4"
- 1 Hemostat Forceps 5.5"
- 1 Triangular Bandage (See Muzzle Instructions)
- 3 Safety Pin

Sprain / Strain
- 1 Instant Cold Pack

Wound Care / Burn
- 1 Irrigation Syringe, 20cc
- 2 Saline Solution, 100ml
- 1 Disposable Skin Stapler, 35 Wide Staples
- 1 Skin Staple Remover
- 3 Triple Antibiotic Ointment
- 6 Antiseptic Wipes
- 2 Alcohol Wipes
- 1 2" Self-Adhering Elastic Bandage
- 1 3" Self-Adhering Elastic Bandage
- 1 2" Conforming Gauze Bandage
- 1 3" Conforming Gauze Bandage
- 4 2" x 3" Non-Adherent Sterile Dressing
- 4 3" x 4" Non-Adherent Sterile Dressing

Bleeding
- 1 QuikClot® Advanced Clotting Gauze, 3" x 24"
- 1 Styptic Pencil
- 1 Nitrile Glove (pair)

Medication
- 4 Antihistamine (Diphenhydramine 25 mg) (Give To Animals Only As Prescribed by Vet)
- 1 Hydrogen Peroxide .75oz. (Induce Vomiting)
- 1 Eye Wash .5oz.

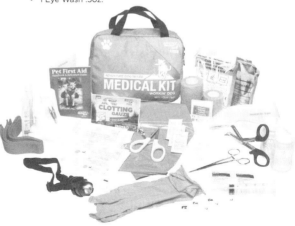

Normal Resting Vital Signs

Capillary Refill

Pink gums and tongue, one second capillary refill time.

To Check: Press gum. Count seconds it takes to return to normal color.

Heart Rate

Heart rate - 50-150

To Check: Feel the pulse in the femoral artery inside the rear thigh. Count the beats for 15 seconds. Multiply by 4.

Respiration

Respiratory rate - 15-30

To Check: Count the number of breaths in 15 seconds. Multiply by 4.

Temperature

Rectal Temperature - 100°-103°

Based in the rugged White Mountains of New Hampshire, Tender Corporation, the maker of Adventure Medical Kits branded products, is one of the largest and most respected medical kit suppliers in the world. The Adventure Medical Kits brand is dedicated to delivering the most innovative products which will keep you safe in the outdoors. Relying on world authorities in wilderness, travel, marine, emergency and now veterinary medicine, Adventure Medical Kits is devoted to delivering the most comprehensive medical kits with up to date medical information to keep you safe on your outdoor adventures. Visit adventuremedicalkits.com for information on our latest products and medical information.

RECORD YOUR DOG'S VITAL SIGNS

Date: **Time:**

1. Respiration:_____breaths each minute (non-panting)

2. Resting pulse or heart rate:_____beats per minute

3. Temperature:_____degrees Fahrenheit

4. Color of Gums:_____

5. Time required for blanched gums to return to normal color:_____seconds

---

Date: **Time:**

1. Respiration:_____breaths each minute (non-panting)

2. Resting pulse or heart rate:_____beats per minute

3. Temperature:_____degrees Fahrenheit

4. Color of Gums:_____

5. Time required for blanched gums to return to normal color:_____seconds

---

Date: **Time:**

1. Respiration:_____breaths each minute (non-panting)

2. Resting pulse or heart rate:_____beats per minute

3. Temperature:_____degrees Fahrenheit

4. Color of Gums:_____

5. Time required for blanched gums to return to normal color:_____seconds

---

Date: **Time:**

1. Respiration:_____breaths each minute (non-panting)

2. Resting pulse or heart rate:_____beats per minute

3. Temperature:_____degrees Fahrenheit

4. Color of Gums:_____

5. Time required for blanched gums to return to normal color:_____seconds

RECORD YOUR DOG'S VITAL SIGNS

Date: **Time:**

1. Respiration:_____breaths each minute (non-panting)

2. Resting pulse or heart rate:_____beats per minute

3. Temperature:_____degrees Fahrenheit

4. Color of Gums:_____

5. Time required for blanched gums to return to normal color:_____seconds

Date: **Time:**

1. Respiration:_____breaths each minute (non-panting)

2. Resting pulse or heart rate:_____beats per minute

3. Temperature:_____degrees Fahrenheit

4. Color of Gums:_____

5. Time required for blanched gums to return to normal color:_____seconds

Date: **Time:**

1. Respiration:_____breaths each minute (non-panting)

2. Resting pulse or heart rate:_____beats per minute

3. Temperature:_____degrees Fahrenheit

4. Color of Gums:_____

5. Time required for blanched gums to return to normal color:_____seconds

Date: **Time:**

1. Respiration:_____breaths each minute (non-panting)

2. Resting pulse or heart rate:_____beats per minute

3. Temperature:_____degrees Fahrenheit

4. Color of Gums:_____

5. Time required for blanched gums to return to normal color:_____seconds